JEFFERSON *vs.* the Patent Trolls

JEFFERSON
vs. the Patent Trolls

A POPULIST VISION OF
INTELLECTUAL PROPERTY
RIGHTS

JEFFREY H. MATSUURA

University of Virginia Press CHARLOTTESVILLE & LONDON

University of Virginia Press
© 2008 by the Rector and Visitors
of the University of Virginia
Printed in the United States of America
on acid-free paper

First published 2008

9 8 7 6 5 4 3 2 1

Library of Congress Cataloging-in-Publication Data

Matsuura, Jeffrey H., 1957–
  Jefferson vs. the patent trolls : a populist vision of
intellectual property rights / Jeffrey H. Matsuura.
    p.   cm.
  Includes bibliographical references and index.
  ISBN 978-0-8139-2771-8 (cloth : alk. paper)
  1. Intellectual property — United States.
2. Jefferson, Thomas, 1743–1826 — Contributions
in law. I. Title. II. Title: Jefferson vs. the patent
trolls.
  KF2979.M34 2008
  346.7304'8 — dc22

                                    2008013579

To Harry and Tomeko Matsuura
for their unwavering support,
to Janice and Anne for their insights
and good humor, and to my old friends
Fuzz, Beau, and Zum

CONTENTS

ACKNOWLEDGMENTS

This book was made possible through the generous support of the Thomas Jefferson Foundation's Robert H. Smith International Center for Jefferson Studies at Monticello. The author would also like to thank the Lemelson Center for the Study of Invention and Innovation at the Smithsonian Institution for the opportunity to participate in its November 2006 symposium "Inventing America."

JEFFERSON *vs.* the Patent Trolls

INTRODUCTION

In today's world we place great emphasis on inventions and other creative works. Intellectual property law rights — patents, copyrights, trademarks, and trade secrets — receive substantial attention. Individuals and nations alike recognize the significant potential economic value of intellectual property rights, having seen over time numerous examples of how inventions and other original works can transform into large profitable businesses and lifestyle-changing products. Intellectual property is widely seen to be a source of economic potential. It is treated as an important asset. There is tension regarding rights of ownership of, access to, and use of intellectual property.

The concept of intellectual property is subject to many different definitions. Viewed from one perspective, intellectual property consists of those forms of tangible and intangible property for which the law grants enforceable proprietary rights. In practice, however, the concept of intellectual property extends beyond the limits of intellectual property law. For example, information and knowledge, although they may sometimes be subject to the formal provisions of intellectual property law, are often places where intellectual property extends beyond the scope of the traditional categories of patents, copyrights, trademarks, and trade secrets.

Our discussion in this book applies this broader notion of intellectual property. It examines Thomas Jefferson's perspective on traditional forms of intellectual property. Yet the book also addresses Jefferson's approach to some of the more expansive and less formal versions of intellectual property, including information and knowledge. We will examine Jefferson's philosophy regarding the significance of the full range of intellectual property forms, including both the property that falls within the scope of traditional intellectual property law and the material that represents the fruit of human creative effort but is not included within the scope of traditional intellectual property law.

It is important to note that Jefferson did not create or express a single comprehensive vision of intellectual property rights. He did not approach intellectual property rights from the perspective of a scholar. Instead, he approached those rights from the perspective of a practitioner. Jefferson was a creator and user of intellectual property. He was also a public servant tasked with granting and overseeing intellectual property rights. As a practitioner, he was interested in fostering both the widespread creation and the use of intellectual property. He faced a wide range of intellectual property rights issues and challenges from a variety of perspectives. His writings and actions in response to those issues and challenges provide helpful insights for practitioners today who also face important intellectual property management questions.

Ours is not the first generation to appreciate the importance of intellectual property. The world of the eighteenth and nineteenth centuries was also transformed by the social, political, and economic impact of inventions and other creative works. That period was also a time, like the present, when perceptions of intellectual property and how it should be managed were evolving. The rise in significance of intellectual property began during that era. It was the first time when attention was paid to the sometimes competing interests of the developers of new works and the users of those works. Thomas Jefferson was an active participant in the efforts to balance incentives for creators of innovative works with broad, rapid public access to those innovative works.

Jefferson's perspective on the significance of intellectual property was far more complete than that of virtually any other major American figure. As a scientist, he understood and respected the critical value of access to information and shared knowledge. As an inventor, he recognized the importance of refinements and enhancements to products and processes. A pioneer patent officer for the United States, Jefferson effectively created the patent review process, at least from an operational perspective. Yet he was also an active consumer of intellectual property developed and controlled by others. In that role, he learned firsthand the frustration encountered by those who depend on the creations of others. If anyone possessed a full understanding of intellectual property rights and their connection with invention and creativity, it was Jefferson.

Jefferson's varied experience with intellectual property is important, not because it illustrates a unified vision of intellectual property rights, but because it provides helpful guidance for practitioners today who struggle with many of the same technology and intellectual property management issues that Jefferson and his colleagues faced. Jefferson expressed his vision of the goals of intellectual property rights, not through a single scholarly thesis, but through an array of actions and various brief written references.

At its core, this book illustrates how the broad perspective Thomas Jefferson developed with regard to intellectual property enabled him to place knowledge, works of invention, and other creative works in their proper place. He recognized that they were essential for the economic prosperity and vitality of this and all other nations. Yet Jefferson also recognized that their impact on American society, and other societies, extended beyond their economic value. He observed that those works were also critical to the political health of the nation. For Jefferson, a healthy democracy required an informed and inquisitive populace. Thus information and works of innovation were a necessary component of healthy political life.

Jefferson recognized another key aspect of invention and creation. He saw them as prerequisites for an equitable social order, and he acknowledged them as the mechanism through which mankind continued its progress toward perfection. A believer in the perfectibility of man, Jefferson viewed the acquisition of knowledge and the application of knowledge to creative, innovative purposes as the engine that drove man's march toward perfection. Intellectual property was more than a collection of assets. It provided the fuel that enabled mankind to drive toward a more just society.

He also saw knowledge and information as critical keys to improving the human condition. The acquisition of knowledge enabled man to come to terms with the forces of nature, harnessing them for the public good. Moreover, information and knowledge were great equalizers, permitting individuals of limited economic means and low social status to take greater control over their lives and to exert influence on the overall form of society. Knowledge empowered the individual and improved the quality of life in the society.

Jefferson's broad experience with the search for knowledge and the quest to apply that knowledge to works of invention and creation enabled him to see that information, knowledge, proprietary intellectual property, and innovation are all connected. In addition, his broad experience allowed him to appreciate that knowledge, intellectual property, and creative works all have profound economic, political, and social impact. This appreciation for the connections between concepts of intellectual property rights and the economic, political, and social aspects of society is perhaps Jefferson's greatest contribution to a philosophy of intellectual property.

If we are to distill the most basic lessons that Jefferson's experience provides for our current debate over intellectual property rights, these are the points to emphasize. We should recognize that knowledge, innovation, and intellectual property are all inextricably linked. We should note further that our decisions regarding policies associated with knowledge, innovation, and intellectual property have critical economic, political, and social consequences. Those consequences should all be evaluated as we establish and implement a framework of intellectual property rights. It is inappropriate and potentially harmful to consider intellectual property rights in a vacuum, isolated from the broader implications of the exercise of those rights.

Jefferson's philosophy favored widespread dissemination of information and knowledge. Shared knowledge provided a firm foundation for political democracy. Shared knowledge also facilitated the continuing invention and innovation necessary to improve the quality of life in a society. Intellectual property rights provided tools to promote the sharing of information and knowledge. Their value rested entirely in their effectiveness in promoting this open exchange of ideas. Intellectual property rights were not goals in and of themselves, but were instead a mechanism through which society attempted to facilitate creative collaboration. They were legal rights intended to encourage acts of creativity and to facilitate rapid integration of the fruits of those acts into useful applications, for the benefit of the society.

Jefferson envisioned a society composed of self-reliant, resourceful individuals. They are independent people, but not deliberately isolated. They have the knowledge necessary to survive and thrive in the natural environment. They possess the observational skills and the aptitude necessary to recognize changes in their environment and to respond to those changes. They are able to communicate and evaluate information, then apply that information to their daily needs. That communication takes place through knowledge networks consisting of both the print media that Jefferson loved so much and the informal conversations and correspondence between individuals. By helping people to develop into active and effective members of these knowledge networks, Jefferson believed that the society would become stronger.

The society that Jefferson envisioned required a dynamic climate of scientific research and the application of that research to social needs. In his society, education played a vital role in the collection and wide dissemination of knowledge. The Jeffersonian society relied on literacy, open inquiry, free communication, and continuing innovation. Intellectual property rights played a role in those essential functions of society, but Jefferson expected them always to facilitate, not to impede, those functions. That sense of perspective has important value as we face the challenges of promoting creativity and innovation today.

For Jefferson, the critical issue was not so much who possessed proprietary rights over intellectual property. Instead, the key factor was who has access to that property and what rights of use are associated with it. He was concerned about a framework of intellectual property rights that enforced a closed, proprietary system for creative works. Such a system, he feared, would impede the search for knowledge and would ultimately slow the application of creative work to pressing public needs.

Instead, he favored an approach that promoted rapid and widespread access to intellectual property. He was willing to offer limited monopoly rights to authors and inventors provided that their works were made accessible to users and other creative individuals. This aspect of Jefferson's intellectual property rights philosophy is highly relevant today. Rights of ownership for innovative works are not nearly as important as rights of use. The critical factor for government to consider as it evaluates intellectual property rights is the extent to which new works, no matter who owns them, are readily accessible to the public.

Yet for all the sophistication of Jefferson's insights into intellectual property and the connections between that property and economic and social forces, he did not effectively recognize the important challenges associated with the transformation of technology into commercial products. Although he had a clear understanding of the technical process through which inventions are created and refined, he did not appreciate the complexity associated with the economic aspects of the evolution of inventions into widely accessible products. For Jefferson, public dissemination of the information and knowledge associated with new technology provided an adequate foundation for commercialization of the technology. Experience has shown that this is not always the case.

Jefferson had a blind spot in his vision of intellectual property. He did not address the economic aspects of invention and commercialization of new technology. As a result, his approach to intellectual property and society was incomplete. While Jefferson emphasized the importance of promoting the process of invention and encouraging the sharing of information, he left it to others to develop the economic and commercial models and transactions that would provide the incentives and opportunities for inventors to convert their innovative work into products available for public use. Only through the creative and diligent efforts of a generation of talented inventors, including James Watt and Eli Whitney, did a model for the commercialization of inventions and new technology emerge. This gap in Jefferson's understanding of intellectual property rights management was not the result of a lack of interest on his part, but instead appears to have been the result of an inability to recognize and appreciate the many commercial challenges associated with the transition from inventive technology to widely used product.

This book does not provide an intellectual history of Jefferson. Nor does it offer an analytical history of patent or other intellectual property rights. It is not intended to provide a detailed examination of either Jefferson or the development of patent and other intellectual property rights. Instead, the book profiles Jefferson as one of the first Americans to be actively involved in all the key facets of intellectual property rights development and enforcement. It examines his writings and actions with respect to intellectual property and inventions in an effort to illustrate how Jefferson, as one of this nation's first major intellectual property rights practitioners, sought to make sense out of the often conflicting opportunities and challenges associated with creation and use of intellectual property. Jefferson serves as a case study for those who, today, work to encourage development of intellectual property and productive management of those creative assets.

Jefferson's experience is helpful, not because he was always right, but because he effectively identified, and attempted to address, the most critical issues in intellectual property rights management. Today's intellectual property rights management professionals face those same practical issues, and Jefferson's experience provides a helpful source of information as they attempt to address effectively the challenge of connecting intellectual property rights with broader goals of economic development and improved quality of life. Jefferson is of interest, and is the focus of this book, not because he presented a comprehensive vision of intellectual property rights, but because he was one of the most active and accomplished practitioners involved with all facets of intellectual property development and use. That breadth of experience made him a leading figure in the field of intellectual property in his time, and it makes him a person of great relevance and value for all who develop, distribute, and use intellectual property today.

Intellectual property rights — legal rights associated with patents, trademarks, copyrights, and trade secrets — are much in the news today. Since these laws form the foundation for technological innovation and associated economic growth, the United States and many other countries around the world currently struggle to enforce intellectual property laws and to modify those rules as necessary to accommodate rapid and dramatic technological advances. The situation is chaotic and unsettled. In this chapter we will review some of the current challenges confronting intellectual property rights management. This chapter places those challenges in historical context, connecting them with similar issues addressed during Jefferson's time. Although the state of our scientific knowledge and the scope of our technology have changed dramatically in the ensuing years, many of the challenges the Founding Fathers faced as they tried to manage the processes of creation, invention, and innovation for the public good remain with us today. For this reason, the practical experience of Jefferson and his colleagues with respect to intellectual property rights management remains highly relevant.

Intellectual property rights provide the legal basis for enabling the creators of original and inventive work to control access to, and use of, those materials. Patent rights are associated with an incredibly wide range of machines, materials, processes, and designs. They provide government-supported monopoly rights to inventors, enabling them to control the manufacture, distribution, and use of their inventions. Copyright protection is provided to original works of authorship, including literary works, music and video recordings, and computer software programs, once those works have been fixed in some tangible form. It controls the duplication, distribution, and exhibition of creative works that have been tangibly expressed. Trademark rights are applied to commercial marks and identifiers that have come to represent and identify, in the eyes of consumers, specific products provided by specific businesses. Trade secret rights are associated with information and knowledge that have commercial value and are protected as proprietary materials by the parties who developed them.

A major part of the challenge of effectively managing intellectual property rights is the fact that the material they govern is often intangible. Although tangible representations of the material exist, the foundation for those tangible assets consists of intangible ideas and insights. Thus, for example, although copyright law protects only the tangible expression of ideas, not the underlying ideas (e.g., the written novel, not the plotline it is based on), those underlying ideas are intangible and highly mobile. Additionally, with today's technology, the tangible asset itself can be converted to electronic form, transmitted, then converted back to tangible form (e.g., online distribution of sound and video recordings). These intricate connections between the tangible and intangible manifestations of intellectual property make it difficult to establish and enforce rational and fair intellectual property rights regimes.

The intangible component of intellectual property connects it to the world of ideas and interpersonal communications. A key aspect of the continuing challenge of effective intellectual property rights management involves the effort to ensure the freedom and accessibility of knowledge and ideas necessary to fuel creativity, while at the same time providing enough proprietary control over the products of the knowledge and ideas to provide economic incentives to encourage transformation of the intangibles into tangible applications.

Today there are important policy challenges with respect to such issues as the extent to which information and knowledge can be proprietary. The complex challenge of determining the extent to which it is appropriate to limit the communication of information and ideas for the sake of protecting proprietary rights associated with intellectual property remains unresolved. There are open questions associated with the extent to which methods of conducting business and other operations (operational practices) should be protected as proprietary intellectual property.

Collectively, intellectual property rights have a profound impact on the creation of original and innovative works. They establish the legal rights available to both the originators and the users of those works. They substantially affect the ability of creators to derive commercial gain from their work. They control the ability of the public to make use of those works. Intellectual property laws provide the legal framework that creates incentives for creation of original works. They also set the terms under which the public can obtain access to those original works. Intellectual property rights set the framework within which creative work is developed and applied.

Today, a great deal of attention is directed to intellectual property rights. Individuals, businesses, research institutions, and governments around the globe are keenly aware of the potential economic value of those rights. Those rights are actively pursued and enforced. Conflicts between owners and users of those rights seem to proliferate daily. Creative works are viewed as important commercial assets. In today's world, they make up a substantial portion of the total value of the global economy, and their share of the world's assets continues to increase at a rapid rate. They are recognized as the materials that drive economic growth and enhance the quality of life. Since it is so highly prized, intellectual property is often the subject of disputes and conflicting claims. The fundamental conflict associated with intellectual property pits the rights of the owners of that property against the rights of users.

Intellectual property rights were viewed differently in Jefferson's time. In the late eighteenth and early nineteenth centuries, there was far less emphasis placed on intellectual property law concepts. Commercial exploitation of intellectual property was a new strategy just beginning to emerge. It was an era dramatically influenced by the principles of the Enlightenment. Methods of scientific inquiry were being formalized. Scientific inquiry, in turn, enabled man to more fully understand nature and mankind's place in the natural order. It was an age of reason, and priority was placed on rational methods of inquiry. Thanks to the insights of Isaac Newton and others, the scientific method of investigation was being widely embraced. It was recognized that man had much to learn about his world, and the scientific method provided the tools to facilitate that learning. Greater emphasis was placed on inquiry and discovery than on control over the knowledge generated by such inquiry.

Jefferson lived in an age of discovery. We too live in an age of discovery; however, our era is also characterized by an emphasis on the ability to control those discoveries. Intellectual property rights provide the key mechanism through which that control is exerted. Several of the most challenging intellectual property rights controversies of today involve, at their core, economic, political, and social concerns that Jefferson and his colleagues understood very well. In Jefferson's time, as in ours, there were ongoing debates about achieving an appropriate balance between proprietary control over intellectual property and promoting the access necessary to encourage continuing creativity and innovation. The factors considered and the methods applied as Jefferson and his peers addressed those concerns are relevant and helpful for us today.

COPYRIGHTS IN THE DIGITAL WORLD

Advances in technology associated with computing, communications, and media have made it easier for virtually anyone to be a creator, distributor, and user of material that is protected by copyright law. In a world of YouTube and peer-to-peer file sharing, thousands of Internet users can copy and distribute copyright-protected material in a matter of seconds, and they can make that material available to millions of people around the world. Users of digital media content have the ability to access that content on a variety of devices. They are also able to make modifications in the original content.

The world of copyright management is far more complex today than it was in Jefferson's time. Jefferson's office of secretary of state served as the first repository of all materials submitted for copyright protection in the United States, a function now performed by the Library of Congress. Although that function was purely administrative, involving collection and retention of copyrighted works, it provided Jefferson with an important role in the operation of copyright law in the early years of this country's existence. On a personal level, Jefferson's love for books brought him into direct contact with the publishing industry, an industry that was both transforming and being transformed by the development of copyright principles. Management of copyrights has been made substantially more challenging today by the technological changes that have taken place in the years since Jefferson was involved with copyrights.

Among the rights granted to creators of original work under copyright law are the rights to copy the work, to distribute it, and to exhibit or perform it. Today's digital media and communications technologies make those basic functions easy to perform and readily accessible to virtually all users of computing devices and the Internet. A wide range of devices now enable users to create digital media files that make text, graphics, images, motion video, and sound recordings compatible with Internet storage and distribution. Anyone can now create their own digital media content and post it on the Internet, making it available to a global audience. Each individual is now capable of being a media content creator and distributor. More troubling, each individual can now easily and quickly find, copy, and redistribute media content created and owned by others.

One response to the rise of the Internet and the associated loss of control over copyrighted material is ever more aggressive enforcement of the legal rights associated with copyright. This approach has been adopted by many media companies, particularly those in the music recording and motion picture industries. These companies actively monitor use of their content online. When unauthorized use of material is discovered, they aggressively enforce their rights of control over the content. This strategy relies substantially on use of the legal system to enforce copyrights. It has led to the somewhat unusual situation in which large media and entertainment companies now routinely take formal legal action against their customers, alleging unauthorized use of copyright-protected content. The result of these enforcement initiatives is nearly daily new reports noting that a music recording company or a motion picture production studio has sued some individual user for copyright infringement.

Enforcement of copyright in digital media continues to become more difficult. As more content is made available in digital format, more people have access to it. In turn, each user can duplicate and share the content, offering it on peer-to-peer file-sharing networks and posting it on Web sites such as YouTube that provide venues for individual users to make content available to other users of the site. Copyright essentially governs the ability to duplicate, distribute, and reuse original works of authorship. The Internet and a wide range of information and telecommunications technologies make those actions highly user friendly. This is the core of the challenge to copyright offered by today's technologies.

An increasingly popular response to the changed environment presented by the Internet and digital media content is the use of open-access strategies. In part, these strategies are based on a realistic assessment of current conditions. Given the capabilities of today's technologies, one must essentially assume that one's intellectual property will be subject to widespread access and use that is not consistent with proprietary control. If people are going to be probing your intellectual property, modifying, it and redistributing it, a realist looks for ways to survive in that changed environment. Open-access strategies provide one set of methods for dealing with the challenges to proprietary intellectual property control.

The most widely known of these approaches is the "open-source" software movement. When computer code is distributed using an open-source license, licensees have the ability to access and modify the source code at the heart of the software. They are free to add to or change the source code in ways that make the software better suit their needs. The only requirement placed on the open-source licensee is that if the licensee chooses to distribute the modified software, the licensee must make its modified version of the source code available on an open-source basis as well. The open-source system provides the software users with the ability to alter, customize, and enhance the software as they see fit. The process thus expands the universe of people who are working to refine the software and to develop applications for it.

In many ways, the open-source system represents the opposite end of the spectrum from the active legal enforcement approach adopted by many content producers. While those who opt for active enforcement believe that approach is necessary to ensure continued respect for copyrights, open-source proponents sense that enforcement alone, no matter how diligently pursued, will not lead to a satisfactory result. Instead, they have chosen to modify their business model, attempting to find ways to provide and extract value in a dramatically changed copyright environment.

Another important digital rights issue is associated with the distinction between intellectual property and information. The basic issue is, at what point does an aggregation of information become a piece of intellectual property? As collections of information develop increasingly significant economic value, there is growing pressure to permit the owners of those data collections to assert legal control over access to their material. Intellectual property law, specifically copyright law, has only limited applicability to such collections of data, since they generally do not constitute the type of original work of authorship that copyrights were established to protect. Collections of information (e.g., databases that aggregate real estate listings or product retail prices) have been deemed by courts to be outside the scope of copyright law protection. Although those works may have substantial commercial value, they are created through the essentially mechanical process of data collection, not human creativity generating original content.

In the past courts had been willing to provide some level of copyright protection for collections of data. Today copyright protection is generally not available. The trend in copyright law is to consider data collections to be works that do not reflect creative initiative, and thus to place them outside the scope of copyright law protection. However, many jurisdictions now provide separate legal protection for data collections, under legal statute. These laws generally give the developers of data collections a legally enforceable right to require economic compensation in exchange for rights of access to and use of their collections. Although technically not a form of traditional intellectual property law, these data protection rights raise interesting legal issues to the extent that they restrict public access to information.

In a world of widespread digital content, there is both active assertion of proprietary rights and broad sharing of content and collaborative content development. One of today's challenges is to balance effectively those two dramatically different philosophies and strategies. Digital rights management is a topic of intense attention all over the world. A major public policy goal is to strike an appropriate balance between rights of content creators and content users. It is difficult to achieve that balance in an environment where technology continues to evolve in ways that extend the capabilities of both content creators and content consumers.

The intellectual property rights challenges presented by the rise of digital media technologies are, at their heart, challenges associated with the empowerment of the individual. Information and communications technologies have made it dramatically easier for people to create, access, duplicate, modify, and distribute media content. Everyone can now be a creator, consumer, and global distributor of media content. Technology evolving to creatively empower the individual is not a process unique to the Internet age. Jefferson was well aware of the ways in which advances in technology can serve to empower individuals. The challenge of effectively balancing often conflicting interests while promoting continuing technological advances was an issue of concern in Jefferson's time, as it is in ours.

In our time, the technologies presenting the greatest disruptive challenge for copyright law are those associated with digital media content creation and distribution. Past disruptive technologies included the development of printing technology that enabled broader creation and distribution of books and other published material. Although Jefferson's generation had no anticipation of a world full of digitized media content, it was well aware of the debates that emerged as authors, publishers, and the public grappled with their often conflicting interests associated with the enhanced capabilities offered by printing technology. Both the print and digital media technology revolutions forced reexamination of the legal rights of creators, distributors, and users of the content generated by those technologies.

Much of the copyright concern expressed in response to the development of digital media technology focuses on the challenge of managing the conduct of individuals to restrain them from misuse of copyright-protected media content. It is also important to ensure that all individuals who legitimately obtain copyrighted material have the opportunity to enjoy that material to the fullest extent enabled by modern technology. Modern technology offers the capability to enhance the enjoyment that individuals can derive from that content, and the law should not unreasonably interfere with that enjoyment. Thus, for example, when digital rights management technology prevents a legitimate buyer of media content from accessing that content through all the different devices the buyer possesses (computer, television, cell phone, personal digital appliance, etc.), the rights of that buyer have been inappropriately constrained. Digital media technology empowers users. Copyright law should not interfere with that empowerment without just cause.

In Jefferson's time, the law associated with rights in original works of authorship was evolving. A transition was then underway, from a common-law notion of works of authorship as property owned by the publishers of that work in perpetuity to statute-based laws that awarded ownership rights of limited duration to the creators of works. That transition reflected a growing recognition of the need to balance the often conflicting interests of creators, distributors, and users of published works. Jefferson and his peers understood the complexity of balancing those competing interests.

In our time, principles of copyright and other legal theories associated with rights of developers, distributors, and users of creative works continue to evolve. Although the technologies associated with those creative works have changed dramatically over the years between Jefferson's time and ours, what has not changed is the complex nature of the challenge associated with encouraging creativity while also ensuring that the results of creative effort will remain accessible for the benefit and enjoyment of the public at fair and reasonable terms. A critical challenge for copyright law in both Jefferson's time and ours is striking the appropriate balance between the rights of content creators and content users. Both groups must have the ability to enforce their rights with respect to copyright-protected works. Achieving that balance was difficult in Jefferson's time and has become even more difficult today.

MANAGING ACCESS TO CONTENT

Computing and telecommunications technologies facilitate immediate and global sharing of information. That capability has incited tension between efforts to manage proprietary material and the free expression and sharing of information and ideas. One example of this tension surfaced in the context of copyright law protections for antipiracy systems and technologies. In an effort to assert their rights under copyright law more effectively, owners of media content now commonly make use of encryption and other technologies to block piracy, the unauthorized use of copyright-protected material. Modern copyright law includes provisions that prohibit initiatives that "circumvent" antipiracy technologies and practices employed by the owners of copyrighted material. Under copyright law today, it is illegal to exercise the rights granted to the copyright owner without permission, and it is also illegal to circumvent antipiracy measures applied by the copyright owner. It is worth noting that current law makes efforts to circumvent copyright protection illegal even if those efforts do not also include actual misuse of the copyright-protected content.

These anticircumvention provisions have been widely enforced. For example, they have been applied to prohibit use of computer programs that remove or impair encryption programs designed to thwart theft of copyright-protected content such as music and video recordings. However, the anticircumvention rules have been interpreted to have quite broad scope. In addition to prohibiting use of circumvention technology, they also prohibit the creation, manufacture, and distribution of such technology. Accordingly, some forms of computer software and other technologies are now treated as contraband simply by virtue of having the capability to defeat technologies that are intended to prevent unauthorized use of copyright-protected material.

Use of the anticircumvention provisions of copyright law to block the distribution of computer software that can override encryption and other copy control programs associated with digital media products introduces a conflict between intellectual property rights and rights of free speech and expression. Under these circumstances, copyright law is used to inhibit development and distribution of certain forms of computer code. Strong objections to this expansive notion of copyright protection have been raised. There is no doubt that copyright holders have the ability to seek compensation when their material has been misused. It is far less clear, however, that they ought to have the right to block the distribution of computer programs that have a variety of uses simply because those programs can be used to override copyright protection measures. Under these conditions, copyright law appears to reach a point where it inhibits creativity and open expression, a result that seems inconsistent with the basic principles behind copyright law.

The debate over the appropriate scope of anticircumvention provisions underscores different perspectives regarding the proper balance between legal requirements and self-help on the part of the parties seeking copyright enforcement. Copyright law provides a legal basis and a process for managing content. Technology, encryption for example, provides operational measures to content owners to manage their property. Some argue that expanded legal measures, such as the anticircumvention provisions of copyright law, constitute an unnecessary extension of legal oversight that unreasonably undermines the rights of content users. Others contend that, given the rapid rate of technology development, anticircumvention provisions are required if the rights granted to content owners are to be enforceable and thus meaningful.

It seems clear, however, that an important line is crossed when copyright protection measures impede access to content. Copyright law has always provided remedies for the misuse of copyright-protected material. Penalties, particularly when those penalties are criminal law penalties as they are in the United States today, applied to actions that do not necessarily involve any direct misuse of copyrighted material constitute a serious extension of the reach of copyright law. This type of extension of the scope of copyright law seems particularly harsh when traditional copyright rules seemed to provide adequate mechanisms for legal relief in the event of copyright infringement resulting from malicious circumvention of antipiracy measures.

Traditional copyright law provided for penalties applicable to parties who facilitate or enable copyright infringement. Indirect and secondary infringement principles have long provided legal mechanisms to sustain copyright actions against those who facilitate or enable copyright infringement. Those copyright law principles could clearly be invoked against parties who enable copyright infringement by providing software and other technical means to circumvent antipiracy systems. The existence of theories of indirect and secondary liability for copyright infringement should make specific anticircumvention provisions unnecessary.

A vital issue at the heart of the topic of management of access to copyright-protected content is the scope of fair use. Copyright law has long been premised on a notion that the system will tolerate limited use of copyrighted material that takes place without permission from the copyright owner. Under the principle of fair use, the law permits a limited amount of duplication, distribution, and exhibition of copyright-protected material even if the owner of the copyright has not specifically authorized such conduct.

According to the principle of fair use, although there is technically infringement of copyrighted material, that infringement is forgiven based on the assessment that the public benefits associated with the use outweigh the likely harm to the owner of the copyright. For example, if an excerpt from an article is duplicated and distributed for use in a course at an academic institution, that use, although technically infringement, will generally be permitted under copyright law. The educational value of the use of the material is deemed to offer broad social benefit, at essentially no cost to the copyright owner. If society were to permit a copyright owner to totally deny access to the protected material, society would be the poorer for that loss of access.

Note that fair use is considered to be a defense against a copyright infringement claim. A user of copyright-protected material does not apply for or request fair-use status. Instead, the user makes its own judgment as to whether the anticipated use will qualify as fair use. After using the material, if the copyright owner believes that the use does not qualify, the copyright owner has the right to sue for copyright infringement. As part of the defense in that infringement action, the user of the material can present evidence to show that the use did qualify as fair use.

Fair use plays a critical role in the continuing efforts to balance proprietary interests with publicly beneficial access to intellectual property. It is a legal concept that tempers the ability of an owner of copyrighted material to exercise unrestricted control over access to that material. Current efforts are underway to help to ensure that fair use continues to be recognized as a fundamental principle of copyright law. The principle of fair use offers an important tool in the effort to balance the rights of copyright owners with the rights of users. It provides a mechanism through which users retain a limited level of access to content even without the prior specific approval of the owner. Fair use provides a method to ensure that proprietary material will remain publicly accessible at least for limited purposes deemed to be in the public interest.

There are also current debates regarding the potential need to extend the concept of fair use beyond traditional copyright law. As discussed previously, some jurisdictions now provide legal rights to the developers of data collections. Although those collections are not generally protected under copyright law, their owners now have separate legal rights to compensation from those who access the content of the collections. Users of the information in those collections note that many of the statutes that provide rights to developers of data collections do not provide for limited fair use of their content. Since the collections are not within the scope of copyright law, the fair-use defense that is always available with respect to copyrighted material is not automatically available with respect to protected data collections. This means that users may have had more rights of access to the data collections if they had been copyrighted than they do now, with those collections having separate legal protection. Some users contend that the public should have the same type of fair-use defense with respect to use of protected data collections.

Nations around the world are at present attempting to strike an appropriate balance between preservation of the integrity of proprietary rights and the unquestioned benefits of the free flow of information and knowledge. This issue is another that was faced in the past. Jefferson and his colleagues were also confronted by the need to devise an appropriate accommodation between open, wide-ranging communication of information and limitations on that information sharing based on principles of proprietary rights and national security. Jefferson's generation was particularly sensitive to government actions that interfered with the open flow of communications and information.

Each generation and each society confronts that challenge and must reach its own conclusions regarding an appropriate balance. All hope to reap the benefits of innovation and growth that come with widespread dissemination of information and knowledge. Those benefits are achieved at a cost, however. Open information sharing is often a highly disruptive process, from economic, political, and social perspectives. Open communication of ideas is highly productive yet equally unsettling. The issue, both in our time and in Jefferson's, is the amount of discomfort our society is willing to bear in exchange for the substantial long-term gains that open knowledge sharing brings.

PATENTS IN THE GLOBAL ECONOMY

Many different nations now recognize the important connection between patents and economic development. Countries, companies, and individuals around the world realize that patent rights provide important incentives for invention. Patents are also essential to ensure that knowledge about innovations moves quickly into widespread application. Grant of patent rights represents a balance between rewards for the inventor and access by users. The award of a patent is essentially a bargain between the government and the inventor.

In exchange for what amounts to monopoly rights enabling the patent holder to stop all other users of the invention, the government is able to publish the information describing how the invention is made and how it works. With that information publicly available, others can integrate the invention into a variety of applications. All such users must, however, satisfy the patent owner, or the owner can enforce the patent against the user through legal action, a patent infringement lawsuit. It is important to recognize that patent rights are, in a sense, negative rights. They enable the owner of the patent to prevent others from using the invention covered by the patent. Yet, grant of a patent does not ensure that the owner of the patent will be able to make use of the patented device without infringing on the rights of another legitimate patent owner.

An important challenge faced today is the rise of overly broad patents. Because patents effectively set the boundaries of the limits of the legal rights of their owners, the broader those rights, the greater reach patent holders have in restricting use of their inventions. When broad patents are issued, their owners have the ability to stop a wider range of uses and users. Carried to an extreme, grant of broad patent rights can make it difficult for inventors and product users to use and refine existing technologies, and to develop new inventions. Overly permissive patent awards can thus impede future innovation. This results in the perverse result that a legal framework that was largely intended to facilitate innovation could, in fact, impede it.

Debate also exists over the subject matter of patents. In the United States, patents are commonly issued for business methods, computer software programs, living organisms, and genetic sequences. Each of those groups of patents has incited substantial controversy over whether it is appropriate to grant patent rights for work in those fields. The wider the range of inventions and works that are eligible for patent protection, the more challenging the research and technology development environment will be. As the number of active patents in a particular field of work grows, it becomes increasingly difficult to conduct research and invention in that field without infringing on the patent rights of others. Patent proliferation can thus impede research and slow the development of new innovations.

Another important modern patent law challenge is the scope of patent enforcement in countries that are in the early stages of economic development. The United States and other economically mature nations place great commercial and political emphasis on intellectual property law. They rely upon consistent enforcement of comprehensive rules of intellectual property. They require the existence and the effective enforcement of intellectual property laws as a prerequisite for most-favored-nations trading status. In order for developing countries to receive access to and benefits from new technology, they are now required to bring their intellectual property laws and enforcement mechanisms up to a minimally acceptable international standard.

Not surprisingly, immature economies commonly have spotty intellectual property rules, and their ability and willingness to enforce those rules are often uncertain. In spite of that uncertainty, however, developing economies rely on access to intellectual property to fuel their economic development and to improve the quality of life for their people. Developing countries desperately need access to the modern technology controlled by the developed nations. Yet, developing nations also aspire to build their own intellectual property base to serve as an engine for continuing future economic development. They need immediate access to the technology of others, while they simultaneously strive to build an indigenous infrastructure that will enable them to create and apply their own intellectual property in the future.

There is inevitable tension regarding intellectual property rights between mature and developing nations. Mature nations want to restrict access to their intellectual property until they are confident that the developing nations have legal and commercial practices robust enough to enforce intellectual property rules. Developing nations seek prompt access to intellectual property, and they view reluctance on the part of the developed world as a form of economic imperialism. This tension has existed though each cycle of international economic development. It was present in Jefferson's time, and it exists today. It seems likely that such tension is an inevitable part of global economic development.

Establishing a fair and effective patent property law regime was a concern in Jefferson's time, as it is today. The fear that issuing too many patents could impair future innovation by limiting the development of new applications for existing technologies and by restricting refinement and enhancement of current technology has been faced by many generations. Patent law and its enforcement evolve over time, often alternating between broader protections favoring patent owners and more limited rights encouraging users.

Some observers believe that in the United States today we are on the brink of a move back toward more limited patent enforcement, having evolved through a period of broad enforcement benefiting patent holders. In contrast, Jefferson lived in an era when the pendulum of patent law enforcement, in the United States and in other parts of the world, was beginning to shift in favor of patent owners. We may currently be at an inflection point in the curve of patent enforcement activity, and perhaps Jefferson lived at another inflection point. In Jefferson's time, the focus was on the commercial potential for patents and the inventions they represent. Today, we are beginning to reconsider that focus.

One critical distinction, however, is that in Jefferson's time the United States was a young, developing nation. The United States was among the nations that looked to expedite their development by obtaining access to the science and technology developed in other, more mature, nations. Various observers have noted that the United States relied at that time on a stream of people and products from Europe to help fuel its movement toward economic maturity. Immigration of engineers and craftsman from Europe, importation of the latest products, and the flow of knowledge and ideas across the Atlantic were all critically important aspects of America's development. Jefferson and his colleagues understood fully the important connection between access to science and technology and economic development. They advocated aggressive measures to ensure effective importation of the most current knowledge and technology from abroad.

Jefferson has been described as acting as a "scientific scout" during his time in Europe. Jefferson searched for European technology and innovations that could be effectively transplanted to the United States. He advocated a focus on smaller, more readily transferable technologies, believing that it was important for America to first obtain those technologies that could be most rapidly moved into widespread use. He thus emphasized turning to Europe for technology related to infrastructure, agriculture, and light industry. In Jefferson's estimation, America was not yet in a position to assimilate all technology available from Europe. In a 1788 letter to John Rutledge Jr., Jefferson suggested that Americans focus on "lighter mechanical arts and manufactures," since they would probably be more accessible and useful for America.

Some observers believe that the United States pursued an even more aggressive effort to bring technology into the country from abroad than that represented by simple scouting. They suggest that the United States was involved in a deliberate campaign of technological espionage during the late eighteenth and early nineteenth centuries. It is suggested that U.S. government officials such as Alexander Hamilton advocated and implemented direct covert missions to obtain European technology, much of it from England, for the purpose of reverse engineering it and introducing it into the U.S. marketplace. Some contend that such a campaign of industrial espionage played a noteworthy role in the development of American industrialization and helped the country create a foundation for its future success in innovation.

Jefferson and his colleagues also worked hard to promote the rapid development of a domestic science and technology base in the United States. They recognized that all developing countries must pass through this phase if they are to mature and prosper. Many of the strategies and priorities that Jefferson and his colleagues devised to promote American access to the world's leading science and technology are being applied today by nations such as Brazil and Thailand.

It seems that the United States had the good fortune of being cast in the role of technology acquirer in an age when intellectual property rules had not yet developed into the extensive network they constitute today. As the United States interacts with developing countries that are eagerly in search of dramatic technology infusion, it would serve us well to remember that America once passed through that phase as well. The evolution from net intellectual property importer to net exporter — a process that has been repeated throughout history — took the United States many years to complete.

This historical perspective should lead the United States to temper the tone, if not the substance, of its debates with developing nations regarding respect for intellectual property rights. All developing countries, in every era, face the same challenge. They must respect and enforce intellectual property rights in order to become part of the international trade and commerce networks; but at the same time, they have every incentive to be less diligent with respect to those rights in order to obtain more affordable versions of necessary products for their people and to give indigenous companies an opportunity to enter industries that are based on intellectual property. Consideration of Jefferson and his era should remind us that the countries trying to manage those conflicting visions of intellectual property rights enforcement today face greater stakes than the United States did in the eighteenth and nineteenth centuries. With the rate of scientific and technological advance and the dramatic continuing growth of the economic impact of intellectual property, developing nations in our time face the grim prospect of falling further behind the developed countries far faster than was the case in Jefferson's time.

PROTECTION OF CULTURAL AND INDIGENOUS KNOWLEDGE

Cultures in all parts of the world have cultivated over time vast collections of indigenous knowledge. That knowledge includes, among other things, the medicinal use of plants, methods of agriculture in regions of severe climate, and arts and crafts with both artistic and functional value. Traditionally, this knowledge was held within the culture that developed it. Communicated from generation to generation in a society, cultural knowledge provided both a link to the past and a basis for useful contributions to the current generation. Often, a society's particular set of cultural knowledge held the key to its survival when confronted with severe environmental conditions. Indigenous knowledge was vital to the society that developed it. Today we recognize that indigenous knowledge also has notable potential value for other societies as well.

With the advent of global communications and travel, there is now far greater mingling of different cultures. That interaction enables societies separated by dramatic gulfs in time, space, and heritage to share, nonetheless, special knowledge that can be useful in diverse cultures. When a modern pharmaceutical company learns of traditional healing methods using a variety of plants, the company is often able to analyze the properties of the plants and develop man-made chemical versions. For example, a consumer product company may learn that a particular tree bark has long been used by various cultures for oral hygiene, and that company can then develop toothpastes and other products that make use of that cultural knowledge.

This sharing and reuse of knowledge across cultures is not a new phenomenon. Cultures have long learned from each other and made use of that transferred knowledge for beneficial applications. The challenging modern twist to this process lies in the significant economic potential of cultural knowledge. If the pharmaceutical company that learns the secrets of the medicinal value of a plant indigenous to the rain forest transforms that knowledge into billions of dollars of profits, and if the company has no obligation to offer any compensation in exchange for that knowledge, the situation can incite controversy, particularly when the society that developed the cultural knowledge is economically poor. The controversy can grow more heated when the pharmaceutical company sells its man-made version of the product in the country that originated the knowledge and when the company is particularly assertive with respect to its patent and intellectual property rights.

Active transfer of cultural and indigenous knowledge also took place in colonial America. Citizens of the young United States borrowed knowledge from the cultures indigenous to this continent, and that process of absorption was a dynamic and well-accepted aspect of development during Jefferson's time. The difference in today's world, again, is the substantial economic value realized by the recipients of that knowledge transfer. Another difference is the apparent asymmetry with respect to the enforcement of intellectual property rights. In the present, economically developed countries are highly active in their efforts to prod developing countries to develop more sophisticated intellectual property rights laws and to enforce those laws more rigorously. From the perspective of many of the developing countries, if there is to be that level of focus on intellectual property rights, then rights on both sides should be enforced equally. If intellectual property from the developed world is to be protected, then the cultural and indigenous knowledge from the developing world should also be actively protected.

BALANCING SECRECY AND DISCLOSURE
IN THE INTERNET AGE

A major challenge confronting our networked society is the effective management of proprietary and public information and knowledge. We are aware of the vast potential social benefits associated with rapid, widespread accessibility to information and knowledge through the Internet. We also increasingly note that such widespread accessibility frequently makes it difficult to protect proprietary material from unwanted disclosure. Modern technology makes immediate global distribution of content a common occurrence. In such a situation, however, it is difficult to prevent content disclosure or to ensure that such disclosure is limited.

The rise of information technologies and the Internet highlighted interesting issues associated with the relationship between intellectual property rights and communications. Debates and controversies surfaced when proprietary rights were applied in ways that appeared to restrict the communication of information. In the context of computer software, for example, there are continuing debates over the nature of computer code. At one level, computer code can be viewed as a mathematical algorithm. It is a series of instructions that cause computing devices to perform a wide range of functions. Viewed from another perspective, however, that same code represents a form of communication. As the case of computer software shows, in an environment where content is commonly proprietary intellectual property, publicly useful information, and a form of communication all at once, challenging intellectual property rights issues emerge.

Copyright law accepts computer code as an original work of authorship fixed in tangible form, and thus provides for legal ownership of the code. Patent law, in the United States, treats code as a patentable invention, provided that the code meets the patenting requirements of utility, novelty, and nonobviousness. Computer code can also be treated as a trade secret, protected from disclosure but not always safe from the process of reverse engineering. Computer code is thus one of the relatively few types of work that is eligible for intellectual property law protection under all the different intellectual property categories.

Yet computer code can also be characterized as an exchange of information. Code provides a means of communicating between humans and computing devices. From this perspective, computer code can be looked upon as a form of communication, as a form of individual expression. Computer programs convey useful information. They are content, information, and communication, all combined together. Looked upon in this light, legal restrictions that limit the distribution of code constitute a form of restriction on communication and individual expression.

Resolution of this debate is beyond the scope of this book. The issue is important, however, since it underscores the evolution of the distinction between intellectual property and communication of information. We now realize that there are instances when assertion and exercise of intellectual property rights may limit and restrain the communication of publicly useful information. Jefferson, too, recognized that there can be such a tension between intellectual property and the exchange of information. Obviously, he did not contemplate computers, the global telecommunications system, and the Internet. He did, however, appreciate the potential for conflict between enforcement of intellectual property laws and the effective communication of information and knowledge. In such circumstances, Jefferson consistently supported promotion of knowledge and information sharing, even if such sharing required less active assertion of intellectual property rights.

The development of the Internet and associated technologies also forces reexamination of our notions of secrecy. It is becoming increasingly difficult to establish and maintain secrecy with respect to information. There is a growing expectation that the duration of secrecy for much proprietary information is becoming more limited. Technological advances are rapidly subjected to reverse engineering that permits others to identify and duplicate those advances. Technology provides both the means to enhance content security and the methods to penetrate that security.

Two important responses to the erosion of secrecy have emerged. One is more aggressive assertion of intellectual property rights for the limited time they are enforceable. The other is application of alternative strategies that do not assume long-term advantage based on any single technological advance. In an environment in which proprietary information cannot be kept secret indefinitely, owners of that information tend to pursue all available legal measures to preserve secrecy, and thus their competitive advantage, for as long as possible. At the same time, however, acting in recognition of the operational realities, the owners of that information develop alternative plans that will enable them to thrive even after the advantages brought by the secrecy of the innovative proprietary information are lost.

These challenges associated with preserving competitive advantage through preservation of proprietary information are not unique to the present. In Jefferson's time, effective management of proprietary material was also becoming more difficult. Inventors such as James Watt, one of the first to deliberately pursue a technology commercialization plan, based on proprietary control of his steam engine technology, faced major challenges establishing and preserving proprietary information. Many different generations, including Jefferson's, grappled with the challenge of providing necessary security for proprietary content while accommodating appropriate communication of publicly valuable information. Although technological advances have made the issue more pronounced in our time, past efforts to achieve an effective balance between closed content and open access have lessons to offer us.

INTELLECTUAL PROPERTY RIGHTS
IN PROPER PERSPECTIVE

One of the important public policy challenges now facing us is the fact that while we have grown to recognize and appreciate the substantial potential economic value of patents and other forms of intellectual property, we appear simultaneously to have lost track of its political and social impact. By examining Thomas Jefferson's willingness to place intellectual property rights in the broader economic, political, and social context, we may be able to assess more accurately the true value of intellectual property to the nations of the world. We may also be better positioned to craft intellectual property policies that more effectively maximize the political and social value of those assets, along with their economic potential.

Intellectual property rights now receive such extensive commercial and political attention that they are often considered in isolation. Patents, trade secrets, and other forms of intellectual property are perceived to be assets, analogous to the tangible assets of land and personal property. They can be bought, sold, and leased. They can also be treated as collateral in exchange for financial loans. Their future earning power can be leveraged into current cash. The direct and powerful link between intellectual property rights and economic growth is widely appreciated.

This attention encourages us to view intellectual property rights as ends in themselves. Instead, intellectual property law and the rights it establishes should be viewed as policy tools. Those tools should be applied to advance important economic, political, and social objectives of the society. Patents, copyrights, trademarks, and trade secrets are important not only because they can generate commercial value but because they can provide a framework conducive to continuing scientific research, technological advances, dissemination of knowledge, and application of innovations to enhance the quality of life. The challenge of recognizing and accommodating the broad role that intellectual property rights play in society is as important today as it was in Jefferson's time.

Jefferson and his colleagues did not isolate intellectual property rights. Instead, their consideration of those rights was part of a broader conversation involving the commercial, political, and social implications of science, education, and creativity. This more comprehensive approach, which treated intellectual property rights as a secondary concern, subservient to the primary objective of promoting public benefits, may be appropriate for our time as well.

The ability of Jefferson's generation to consider intellectual property rights as a component of a broader strategy for public welfare and advancement was likely assisted by the circumstances of the day. There was then no widespread use of intellectual property rights as the basis for commercial competitive advantage, although that situation was certainly changing during Jefferson's lifetime. As a result, there was far less pressure being placed on the intellectual property rights framework by commercial interests than is present today. Even so, the care exercised by Jefferson and his peers as they sought to promote the rights of authors and inventors while also preserving necessary public access to the works of creators can be instructive for us today.

EROSION OF THE PUBLIC DOMAIN

The public domain consists of all works that are not eligible for intellectual property law protection, materials that were once protected by intellectual property law but are no longer so protected, and those that have been donated to the public domain by their creators. The public domain contains, for example, much of the work created and released by governments (e.g., government reports and other government publications). It also contains inventions for which the patents have expired and copyrighted works whose terms have ended. Trademarks that are abandoned and those that become "generic" terms through inadequately restricted use (e.g., "aspirin") are also part of the public domain.

Public domain material can be used by anyone. Use of public domain material raises no legal liability. There is no obligation on the part of the user of the material to compensate anyone. The concept of the public domain is that it provides a pool of material that can be used and reused by anyone. We see examples of the impact of the public domain every day. For example, the vintage video and motion picture excerpts that find their way into commercial advertising often consist of material that has come off copyright protection. Music compositions that are repackaged into other works often consist of material that was created prior to the existence of copyright protection or for which copyright protection has expired. When patented drugs come off patent, many different manufacturers can create and distribute similar versions of the original patented product. The public domain provides a rich, diverse, and important repository of creative components that can be modified, enhanced, and repurposed for commercial gain and the public good.

There is much debate today on the issue of whether the public domain is being unreasonably limited. One contention is that as intellectual property rights become broader and more extensive, there is a risk of choking off the public domain. For instance, over the relatively recent past, U.S. copyright law was amended on more than one occasion to extend the term of copyright protection. Those rights now extend for decades after the original creator of the work has died. Some argue that these very long intellectual property rights terms unreasonable restrict the public domain. There is concern that those restrictions may ultimately harm the society by impeding the rate of innovation.

In today's environment, there is some reason to fear that the public domain may become unreasonably limited through overly broad intellectual property rights. In Jefferson's time, the public domain provided an important resource. Many decades of increasingly assertive intellectual property rights policies and strategies have placed limitations on the public domain that were not present when Jefferson lived. Although technology has made public domain material readily accessible to people all around the world, the broad assertion of intellectual property rights threatens to limit the volume of public domain material.

In Jefferson's time, the public domain was a resource that was essentially taken for granted. His views and activities regarding intellectual property were, in large measure, the product of living in an age when the public domain was broad, and the concept of active proprietary rights claims limiting the scope of the public domain was not yet dominant. An avid believer in the importance of shared knowledge, Jefferson relied on the public domain as a source of ideas and opportunities for future innovations and advances. The challenge of preserving the public domain was far less of an issue in Jefferson's time, but he was mindful of its importance. Just as he favored an agrarian vision of America's future in which individuals directly tapped the vast land resources of this country, Jefferson had a similar vision regarding intellectual property. That vision included a vast and growing public domain of creative content and knowledge to be tapped by individuals pursuing the innovations and insights that would enhance America's future.

Even in Jefferson's time, however, the seeds for potential erosion of the public domain were clearly present. The first statutory establishment of copyright protection took place in England in 1709 with the enactment of the Statute of Anne. Prior to that legislation, the dominant legal theory applied to works of authorship was a common-law approach based on that applied to land. Under that approach, publishers of printed material claimed a perpetual ownership right in their published works. The Statute of Anne created set terms for ownership of published works (twenty-one years for books already in print at the time of enactment and fourteen years for works published after enactment).

The concept of a perpetual ownership interest in works of authorship, based on common law, was overridden by the Statute of Anne and subsequent copyright legislation. Yet that common-law heritage provided the basis for continuing efforts to extend the scope of proprietary interests in works of authorship. Extension of those proprietary interests reduces the scope of the material available in the public domain. The conflict over the scope of the public domain has been waged from before Jefferson's time up to the present. The challenge of protecting and managing the public domain is a modern issue with roots that extend back through Jefferson's time.

An extensive and open public domain is a key component of the dynamic, collaborative process of innovation preferred by Jefferson. The public domain is the forum in which information and knowledge are shared. It is the venue for expressing, testing, and modifying ideas. In a very real sense, the public domain provides the components from which the inventions of the future are built. It is the natural resource that fuels creativity and innovation. The public domain was an important public resource in Jefferson's day, it continues to be so today, and it will be an essential asset in the future. Jefferson understood that, and it is in the public interest for us as well to appreciate the value of the public domain.

TWO

JEFFERSON AND
THE VALUE OF SHARED
KNOWLEDGE

A critical factor associated with the development and use of intellectual property is access to knowledge and information. Intellectual property rights both limit and rely upon sharing of knowledge and information. Patents, copyrights, and other forms of intellectual property law sustain the sharing of information and knowledge by providing a legal framework that establishes the terms of access to and use of much of that material. Yet intellectual property law can also impede the free exchange of information to the extent that it enables developers of knowledge to restrict rights of access and use. The challenge of balancing restriction and free flow of that material is an important issue today. It was also of critical significance in Jefferson's time. Jefferson directed much attention to promoting the development and sharing of knowledge. In this chapter we examine his views on the subject of dissemination and use of knowledge.

THE SIGNIFICANCE OF KNOWLEDGE SHARING

For Jefferson, a cornerstone of an effective democracy was the ability to disseminate knowledge and information widely among its citizens. While a member of the Virginia General Assembly in 1778, he authored "A Bill for the More General Diffusion of Knowledge." In that legislation Jefferson took the position that the most effective means to fight tyranny was "to illuminate, as far as practicable, the minds of the people at large." In effect, shared knowledge was, for him, a key component of a healthy society. Jefferson was unable to persuade the Virginia General Assembly to enact the legislation. Nonetheless, years later, he wrote to George Wythe that he believed that the 1778 legislation was "by far the most important bill in our whole code." He asserted that widespread knowledge was essential to democracy, and that "no other sure foundation can be devised for the preservation of freedom and happiness." His efforts to win passage of this legislation provided an early indication of his lifelong interest in, and concern for, the expansion of educational opportunities.

Jefferson's respect for the social and political significance of widespread knowledge can be traced to several different sources. In part, that respect links Jefferson to a rich tradition in French political thought — one of whose leading proponents was Condorcet — that embraced the notion of the perfectibility of man. This tradition was built on the principle that, through the acquisition of information and knowledge, man could improve his social condition. Through education and shared knowledge, too, quality of life could be improved and nations could attain and preserve democratic ideals. For Jefferson, the key to continuous improvement of the human condition was the extension of knowledge. The pool of knowledge must be continually expanded and access to that pool must be provided to an ever-growing segment of the population, with the goal that eventually all members of the society, rich and poor alike, should have access to the vast collection of human knowledge.

Jefferson's emphasis on education and publicly accessible knowledge were also linked to his concept of dynamic societies governed by vibrant republican governments. Influenced by elements of the republican internationalist movement of the eighteenth century, Jefferson believed that the republican form of government provided an ideal social foundation, and he expected that nations around the world would adopt that form of government over time.

For Jefferson, the goal of education was not the mere collection of facts. He believed that the French encyclopedists adopted too limited a notion of knowledge. In his estimation, large collections of information did not translate directly to knowledge or wisdom. Collected information must be combined with analysis and experience to be of true value. Education is the process through which information is distributed and analytical methods are ingrained. Education provides information, but it also helps to cultivate knowledge.

Ideas, for Jefferson, were meant to be shared widely. Writing to Isaac McPherson in 1813, he noted that "if nature has made any one thing less susceptible than all others of exclusive property, it is the action of the thinking power called an idea." Once expressed by its creator, an idea "forces itself into the possession of everyone, and the receiver can not dispossess himself of it." Perhaps the most important characteristic of ideas "is that no one possesses the less, because every other possesses the whole of it." Ideas are meant to be shared, and once they are shared, no one receives less value from the idea simply because other people also possess it.

In Jefferson's judgment, "he, who receives an idea from me, receives instruction himself without lessening mine." Ideas are like flames, and "he who lights his taper at mine, receives light without darkening me." Jefferson noted that ideas are "expansible over all space, without lessening their density in any point." Most important, ideas, "like the air in which we breathe," are "incapable of confinement or exclusive appropriation."

His correspondence with McPherson offers a clear illustration of his view of knowledge. Knowledge, for Jefferson, is not private, personal property. It is, instead, a communal asset, open and accessible to all. All may contribute to the pool of knowledge, and all may draw from it. From an intellectual property rights perspective, this is the classic description of the public domain. For Jefferson, the public domain is critical to the intellectual vitality of a society. Indeed, the importance of the public domain extends beyond the theory of knowledge. In Jefferson's view, the public domain is the venue in which knowledge is shared, ideas are tested and refined, and the process of transforming theory into practical applications that can sustain and enhance human life begins.

The networked aspect of knowledge was very important to Jefferson. Throughout his life, he cultivated and communicated with networks of leading thinkers in science and philosophy. He did not hesitate to consult with those networks when he had a question to resolve or when he wanted to test and refine his thoughts. He was also an active participant in those networks, providing comments and insights in response to the inquiries of others. His active participation illustrates his respect for the intelligence of communities. Although Jefferson clearly valued the intelligence of the individual, he recognized that a network of thoughtful individuals could provide more intellectual power than even the most brilliant individual acting alone.

Jefferson's reliance on knowledge networks also highlights his recognition of the evolutionary aspect of knowledge. Knowledge is derived as facts are gathered and evaluated, theories are proposed and tested, and ideas are developed and challenged. All these stages in the process of knowledge development function more effectively when the resources of a network of people are available. Jefferson relied on his knowledge networks to keep him current on the state of affairs in a wide range of fields. He actively used those networks to help himself clarify, refine, and extend his thoughts on virtually any subject. In today's information technology industry, there is widespread appreciation for the power of networks. Jefferson recognized that power in his time as well.

Observers have noted that Jefferson's greatest value to the world of thought was not necessarily his original ideas and insights but, instead, his substantial ability to serve as an intellectual sounding board for the leading issues and ideas of the time. Jefferson was thus ideally suited to function as an active leader of the thought networks of his era. The connections linking Jefferson's knowledge network were slower and more cumbersome than those made possible by today's modern information and communication technologies. Nevertheless, he relied on knowledge networks, and he was a widely respected member of those communities. In a very real sense, Jefferson and his colleagues anticipated the vast knowledge networks that modern technologies now enable.

Jefferson's respect for networks of knowledge was not limitless. He had great respect for those who cultivated knowledge, but disdain for those who were poorly informed. One can imagine that Jefferson would welcome the opportunities to create networks of knowledge afforded by the Internet and other modern communications technologies. One might also speculate that he would be seriously concerned that networking technology carries the potential to empower individuals who are ignorant and malicious. While it is likely that he would applaud modern technology to the extent that it facilitates creation of communities of knowledge, it is equally likely that he would be deeply disturbed by the potential those same technologies possess to provide a broad platform for the voices of ignorance.

It is interesting to consider that the environment we now face in our Internet-connected world might underscore some of the contradictions present in Jefferson's perspective on the role of the intellectual elite and the potential of the general public. In our current networked society, we have substantially created a global system that enables instantaneous communication, the sharing of information and ideas. That infrastructure provides important support for the rapid exchange and enhancement of many important and useful ideas. That same infrastructure also enables global dissemination and embrace of the most venomous and unfounded lies and misconceptions. It provides a vital tool in support of intelligent, reasoned interaction on the one hand, and hateful, irrational vendettas on the other. Jefferson believed in the perfectibility of man, based on man's limitless ability to learn and to improve. At the same time, he recognized and was repelled by man's weaknesses and failings. Modern technology amplifies both aspects of our personality as a species. One assumes that Jefferson would not be surprised by this result. It would be fascinating, however, if one could know his reaction to it.

For Jefferson, ideas and knowledge were public property. No single individual ever served as the solitary developer of an idea or the sole source of knowledge. Instead, knowledge was accumulated through the collective actions of many different people in many different places over extended periods of time. Ideas are to be tested, refined, and advanced as they are shared among a variety of individuals. There is no point to efforts to assert proprietary control over ideas or knowledge. An idea that is not disclosed has no value, since it can never be developed, tested, extended, or applied. Once disclosed, knowledge and ideas take on lives of their own, independent of those who originally shared them. As each idea is shared, modified, and applied by many other people, the idea grows in value. Ideas do not lose value as they are shared; instead, they gain value. And once they are expressed, ideas cannot be confined or constrained. They cross geographic boundaries, and they span eras of time. Knowledge is timeless and enduring.

One of the reasons that Jefferson so treasured his membership in the global community of scientists was his sense that it was one of the very few communities, the community of artists being another, in which information continued to be shared even when political forces shattered other lines of communication. A member of the Agricultural Society of Paris, Jefferson noted that both he and the Duke of Bedford in England received a new French design for a plow in 1809. That information had been disseminated by the society with the deliberate intent of ensuring that the new design promptly be made available to farmers in the United States and England. Jefferson noted that this distribution of information between France and England took place even though those two countries were then at war. Jefferson noted that science "societies are always in peace, however their nations may be at war." He added that the world's science communities "form a great fraternity spreading over the whole earth" and "their correspondence is never interrupted by any civilized nation."

Jefferson embraced the traditional vision of the scientific community that information and ideas should reside in the public domain, that vast and ever-growing repository of the sum of human knowledge. That repository provided, in Jefferson's view, the components from which new knowledge and future applications would be developed. It was, and should always be, a public resource, openly accessible to all. Implicit in this view is an assumption that there are no personal property rights associated with knowledge and ideas. Attribution of ownership is a meaningless concept, since knowledge merges the work and creativity of many people in many places over a vast expanse of time.

Inherent in this vision of a community of informed individuals creating networks of knowledge is some degree of conflict with basic intellectual property rights principles. Traditional intellectual property law, with its emphasis on proprietary content and controlled access, often conflicts with the vision of knowledge sharing that Jefferson embraced. As Jefferson extended his activities in the world of traditional intellectual property law development and enforcement, he always retained his respect and appreciation for the importance and value of shared knowledge and information. His views on intellectual property law and his actions as he enforced those laws were influenced and tempered by his faith in the power of knowledge sharing. Jefferson consistently placed greater emphasis on making knowledge and know-how widely accessible than on honoring rights or proprietary control.

THE VALUE OF THE SCIENTIFIC METHOD

Jefferson was a firm believer in the value of the scientific method of inquiry. He recognized the significance of the methodology and process used to define, analyze, and address questions and problems. Embracing the scientific method developed by pioneers like Newton, he favored quantitative analysis over qualitative analysis whenever possible. Further, he sought to use the principles of scientific analysis to examine issues of politics, governance, and social concerns, not just traditional scientific fields. Jefferson's acceptance of this approach to inquiry and investigation places him well within the traditions of the Enlightenment.

For Jefferson, scientific inquiry begins with an effort to define the question to be addressed. After effective definition of the question, one could outline a plan of research and analysis that would yield useful data. The process of acquiring relevant data involved both research of existing information and collection of new data through experimentation and disciplined observation. After data have been collected, they must be reviewed and analyzed. That analysis could generate additional questions, suggest modifications to the original inquiry, and provide a basis for developing answers to the original question.

In Jefferson's estimation, merely developing an answer was not sufficient. Care must be exercised in defining the question and in devising experiments and research that could yield useful data.

Collection of that data required diligence, patience, and discipline. Analysis of the data required intellectual rigor, and a willingness to test results and to reconsider them. Even after an answer was obtained, the process required a willingness to test and retest the validity of the answer. New data must continuously be obtained, and those new data must be introduced into the analytical process. Ultimately, Jefferson had faith in the ability of the process of scientific inquiry to address effectively all challenges confronted by mankind.

Jefferson's high regard for the scientific method was shared by others who embraced the rational values and the search for reason that were key attributes of the Enlightenment. His emphasis on a disciplined, rigorous process of inquiry and analysis profoundly influenced both his concept of knowledge and his conduct in all spheres of his life. This generous appreciation for the process of inquiry highlights a significant aspect of Jefferson's view of knowledge. For Jefferson, knowledge was not merely a collection of information and facts. Of critical importance to him was the process for acquiring knowledge. The process of scientific inquiry provided the continuing means of refining and extending human knowledge.

THE ESSENTIAL ROLE OF EDUCATION

Education was the process through which all citizens would learn about the content of the vast pool of knowledge and how to access and process that pool in a meaningful way. Education also provided the vehicle through which each generation would learn how to use the scientific method of inquiry and investigation. Education was, for Jefferson, a critical component of democracy. It was vital to the development of an informed public, and only with an informed public could a nation survive as a vibrant democracy.

In pursuit of his goal of universal education, Jefferson advocated the creation of a national university for the United States. Ultimately, that effort led to the creation of the University of Virginia. The university was intended by Jefferson to function as an academic community where education was available, not based on wealth or privilege, but on merit and thirst for learning. In an 1800 letter to Joseph Priestley, Jefferson summarized his key goals for the university he sought to establish. He observed that the leading objective was "to establish an University on a plan so broad and liberal and modern, as to be worth patronizing with the public support, and be a temptation to the youth of other states to come and drink of the cup of knowledge and fraternize with us."

Jefferson believed that a national university was necessary to provide a quality liberal education to the nation's youth. He wanted the university to help create a population that could effectively retain and enhance the nation's democratic values. Jefferson anticipated a curriculum including the following subjects: "Botany, Chemistry, Zoology, Anatomy, Surgery, Medicine, Natural Philosophy, Agriculture, Mathematics, Astronomy, Geology, Geography, Politics, Commerce, History, Ethics, Law, Arts, Fine Arts." He considered it important to attract some of the leading scientists from Europe to teach at the university, and he expected to require the faculty to devote their full time to teaching and research.

Some question the depth of Jefferson's commitment to free and open thought, even in the context of institutions of higher education. Jefferson was not prepared to rely solely on academic and intellectual merit with regard to faculty appointments, for example. He was willing to include political considerations in decisions regarding the hiring of faculty and administrators. Jefferson's vision of institutions of higher education certainly portrayed them as sites of active intellectual inquiry, but such inquiry also took place within the context of political requirements. Although a believer in the importance of open and wide-ranging research inquiry, Jefferson was not above limiting the freedom of that academic inquiry, at times, for political reasons.

Jefferson's belief in the power and value of education also surfaced in his support for the creation of the United States Military Academy at West Point. Jefferson believed that there was a growing need for a corps of trained engineers to support American military operations. He believed further that such a cadre of professional engineers would prove valuable not only for military purposes but also in support of the civilian needs of the growing country. Jefferson wanted West Point to serve as the training ground for the professional engineers who would lead this country in war and peace. Although the institution would focus on training technical professionals for the military, Jefferson believed that the long-term benefits of that education would be reaped by American society as a whole.

The strength of Jefferson's commitment to the scientific and technical focus of West Point was underscored by the selection of the academy's first superintendent, Jonathan Williams, a grand-nephew of Benjamin Franklin. Williams's connection to science extended as far back as childhood, when he assisted Franklin in conducting experiments on the Gulf Stream during a 1785 voyage from Europe to America.

Jefferson's recognition of the importance of education to society was not confined to university-level instruction. He understood the importance of a complete progression of education throughout a lifetime. His effort, ultimately unsuccessful, to have Virginia adopt legislation promoting the general diffusion of knowledge was a comprehensive legislative effort. The educational framework he proposed ranged from early education through the university level. Jefferson believed that early education would have the greatest benefit for society, but he viewed the entire range of educational opportunities as important elements of the long-term and continuing process of learning that is vital to the creation and preservation of a stable democratic society.

In Jefferson's estimation, educational systems should do more than merely provide large quantities of facts and information to students. Educational systems should also teach students the methods of conducting reasoned inquiries into important issues. Using these methods, students would be in a position to resolve critical challenges they would encounter during their lives. Education should not merely catalog facts but must also provide the means to examine and resolve practical problems. For Jefferson and many of his peers, the process necessary for effectively addressing all manner of life challenges was essentially the scientific method of inquiry.

Educational institutions introduced young people into the key knowledge networks of the nation and the world. Their primary value was in empowering each new generation by connecting it to the knowledge that has been acquired over time, and by teaching each generation the fundamental methods of inquiry that would enable it to deal effectively with the new challenges and questions it would meet in the future. Educational institutions would, in Jefferson's estimation, also serve as venues for the creation of new knowledge. They would play active roles contributing to the common pool of knowledge.

THE SIGNIFICANCE OF EXPLORATION

The restless and relentless pursuit of knowledge was an important aspect of Jefferson's vision. Exploration was, for him, a critical aspect of the efforts of mankind to understand nature and man's place in nature. He was a consistent proponent of exploration and dissemination of the knowledge gained from exploration. Jefferson believed that exploration, to be conducted properly, should be performed in a manner consistent with other forms of scientific inquiry. Accurate and complete observation generating reliable data should be at the heart of any exploratory expedition. Explorers should be, at least in part, scientists.

Thus for Jefferson, exploration was more than an adventure or a means of claiming territory. In addition, journeys of discovery were also experiments that could yield important knowledge of the natural world. As such, expeditions required scientific preparation and attention to the methods of scientific inquiry. There is no better illustration of this aspect of Jefferson's character than his unyielding support for the Lewis and Clark expedition exploring the American West.

Although it was clearly a mission with critical economic and national security components, Jefferson insisted that one of the fundamental goals of the expedition was the acquisition of knowledge regarding the people, places, and natural history of the regions to be traversed. In his 1803 written instructions to Meriwether Lewis outlining the goals of the mission, Jefferson noted that the expedition should make observations on plant and animal life, soil, minerals, and climate. The mission was instructed to take navigational sightings and survey land. And of course Jefferson, the paleontologist, also directed the team to note fossil remains they might encounter.

Jefferson took the unusual step of preparing Lewis and Clark for their role as explorers by facilitating their training in diverse fields, including botany, astronomy, and geology, to ensure that their observations and findings would be accurate and provide useful additions to the inventory of general knowledge in those fields. He arranged for special tutoring of Meriwether Lewis in advance of the expedition's departure. Lewis was tutored in several different scientific fields by leading scientists who were also friends of Jefferson, including Benjamin Barton, Caspar Wistar, Robert Patterson, and Benjamin Rush. Jefferson relied on his extensive network of scientific resources to help prepare the Lewis and Clark party for the scientific aspects of their journey. In effect, Jefferson introduced Lewis, and through Lewis, the entire expedition team, to the ever-growing knowledge network of which he was so actively a part.

This preparation illustrates the extent to which Jefferson emphasized the scientific potential of the expedition. Lewis and Clark were to engage in scientific exploration. They would make observations and document them, collect specimens, and survey the territory they were exploring. For their data and observations to have meaning, the team had to develop proficiency in scientific field work. The tutoring was aimed in part at providing the expedition with basic understanding and literacy in the relevant scientific fields, including botany, biology, navigation, meteorology, and geology. That training was also intended to help the team understand and develop proficiency with regard to the process of scientific inquiry, including making accurate observations and documenting those observations precisely and clearly. It also involved understanding the process of collecting, preserving, and protecting specimens for future study.

Jefferson's emphasis on the scientific components of the journey paid substantial dividends. The Lewis and Clark expedition made and documented many important discoveries and observations. Jefferson was highly pleased by the scientific results of the team's voyage. His zeal for the enterprise's ability to add significantly to the inventory of knowledge of the continent was largely embraced by the members of the Lewis and Clark party as well. Their dedication to the scientific aspects of the trip is reflected in the diligence with which they documented their travels. It is also clearly illustrated by the courageous efforts made by the team members, on various occasions, to ensure that their records and specimens were protected and preserved, even when those efforts placed them at personal physical risk.

After the Lewis and Clark party successfully completed its mission of exploration and discovery, Jefferson insisted that the knowledge gained during the party's travels be made widely available. He encouraged the dissemination of the scientific observations made by the team in an effort to advance the state of knowledge in botany, geology, and biology. Jefferson was proud of the expedition and its contribution to the state of knowledge in a variety of different fields.

This eagerness to include scientific exploration as part of the mission of the Lewis and Clark expedition is an important illustration of the priority Jefferson placed on the search for knowledge. By including science in the mission, Jefferson emphasized that the acquisition of knowledge was a national priority on a par with the goals of national security and commercial development. It illustrates his willingness to integrate scientific objectives into the full range of national initiatives. For Jefferson, science was not a separate arena of activity, but an integral part of the commercial, political, and social life of the nation. He took advantage of virtually every opportunity to increase the nation's understanding of science, including reservation of a portion of missions of exploration for the collection of scientific data and observations.

THE DRIVE FOR APPLICATION OF
KNOWLEDGE TO MEET HUMAN NEEDS

Jefferson firmly believed that knowledge should be practical in nature. Man seeks to understand the world around him so that he can improve the human condition. Knowledge has its greatest value when it is applied to meet practical needs. Knowledge in the service of mankind was Jefferson's primary goal. The critical challenge for mankind is to cultivate effective connections between the ever-expanding pool of knowledge and the critical needs of the society. Jefferson fervently believed that essentially all new knowledge would eventually yield practical value. Although a single piece of knowledge, alone, is never sufficient to support practical applications, the collective aggregation of knowledge, spanning different regions and eras, provides the basis for a virtually limitless range of useful applications. The desire always to connect knowledge with practical applications and advances was a vital aspect of Jefferson's personality.

As the boundaries of knowledge are continually extended, every effort must be made to transform that knowledge into applications that have meaningful impact on the quality of life of the public. Mankind's efforts to understand nature must remain coupled with efforts to apply that understanding to uses that are relevant to the critical needs of people. Although he emphasized the need to apply knowledge to practical uses, Jefferson was also patient, recognizing that the development of those useful applications was the result of an evolutionary process that commonly extended over long periods of time.

Jefferson appreciated the way in which knowledge was accumulated by a society. Each member of society, and each generation, built upon the work of others to expand and refine the society's overall understanding of the world and mankind's place in it. He embraced the notion that knowledge, once acquired, could not be lost if it was effectively communicated and shared. In a 1799 letter to William Green Mumford, Jefferson wrote that "what is once acquired of real knowledge can never be lost." Part of the importance of the pursuit of knowledge is that it provides advances for society that remain in perpetuity.

Sharing and dissemination of knowledge thus had multiple purposes. At one level, sharing enabled many different individuals to stay current and to contribute their insights to advance the common knowledge. At another level, knowledge sharing facilitated the testing of ideas, driving improvement in the accuracy and effectiveness of the pool of knowledge. And at yet another level, the sharing of knowledge helped to ensure that advances would not be lost over time. Once knowledge becomes part of the common pool, it cannot be taken away by a tyrant or forgotten. Knowledge thus connects people across geographical and temporal gulfs.

This dynamic suggests a perpetual movement toward improvement of the human story. This philosophy is consistent with Jefferson's willingness to embrace Condorcet's vision of the perfectibility of man. For Jefferson, improvements in the quality of life for the people of a society were the result of advances in knowledge. Knowledge thus had a direct and critically important connection with the public. Man should continue to build his foundation of knowledge, not merely for the sake of intellectual curiosity, but more importantly for the sake of improving the condition of the society.

At their essence, ideas and knowledge were, for Jefferson, public assets. They were communal property to be widely disseminated and always applied for the public benefit. They were not to be hoarded as the exclusive property of any single society or class in a society. Ideas and knowledge were public assets that had value that extended beyond the basic economic perspective. They were forms of intellectual property, but they were not proprietary to any one person, organization, or nation. A society in which ideas are effectively promoted and disseminated is a society that can effectively maintain a democratic political structure. It is also a society in which the citizens have the opportunity to improve their condition. Education is a great equalizer.

Knowledge can provide economic, political, and social opportunities for people who have traditionally been disadvantaged. For Jefferson, it was important to promote education, as well as the cultivation and widespread sharing of new ideas, for economic, political, and social purposes. The significance Jefferson placed on education is clear in his actions and writings throughout his life. There is perhaps no clearer indication of his belief in the importance and power of education than his decision to include his role in the creation of the University of Virginia as one of the three accomplishments memorialized on his grave.

In Jefferson's estimation, information collected through direct observation and communication with others formed the foundation for knowledge. Knowledge was collected and disseminated through the educational system and through other diverse institutions of society. This network of information gathering and rigorous analytical review formed the base for a dynamic society, a healthy democracy, and truly humane community. Shared knowledge was thus the cornerstone of society, and Jefferson worked diligently to promote widespread appreciation for its significance.

Driven by this vision of the economic, political, and social value of shared knowledge, Jefferson possessed a decidedly modern perspective. Today, great emphasis is placed on the significance of knowledge sharing. Our modern technology enables such sharing to an extent unimaginable in Jefferson's time. Jefferson and his colleagues embraced the same concept all those many years ago, and we continue to benefit, as a people, from their insight.

KINDRED SPIRIT
TO SCIENTISTS AND
INVENTORS

J efferson was at home among scientists and inventors. He shared their inquisitiveness and spirit. Observers noted that only Jefferson and Theodore Roosevelt, of all past American presidents, can reasonably be characterized as men of science. Both men shared a seemingly limitless passion to understand the natural world. Much of Jefferson's self-image centered on his appreciation for scientific inquiry. In his time, science was often viewed as synonymous with the pursuit of knowledge. Experimental science and scientific observations, as we know them today, were commonly characterized as "natural history" and "natural philosophy." Jefferson's appreciation for science and the process of formal inquiry are directly connected with the great value he placed on knowledge.

Perhaps Jefferson's greatest contribution to the world of science was his ability to bridge the scientific community and the community of public affairs. He, and several of the other Founding Fathers, worked to connect science with the practical affairs of governance. That connection played an important and beneficial role in the early development of the United States.

Jefferson understood the distinction between science and technology. He appreciated both the fundamental inquiries into nature of the science of his time and the diverse efforts to develop and use technology, generated by science, for applications that benefited the public welfare. He welcomed and supported both basic science and the efforts to apply the fruits of basic science to improve the human condition. One of the reasons he was such an active supporter of shared knowledge and of open access to technical innovations was his recognition that openness is a prerequisite for both scientific and technological advances.

An active and well-known member of the scientific community, Jefferson was elected to membership in America's leading scientific organization, the American Philosophical Society, in 1780. The APS was founded in 1743 to provide a forum in which members of the community could study and discuss science and its practical applications. Although the society lapsed for a time, by 1767 it had recaptured its vigor and developed into an organization that promoted and supported inquiry in a diverse range of fields. The APS provided a forum for discussion and inquiry regarding important issues of science and technology. Its focus on the practical applications for science reflected the emphasis that Benjamin Franklin and the other founders of the organization placed on connecting science and technical knowledge with the public needs of the day.

Jefferson was elected president of the APS in 1797. His term as the APS president coincided with a portion of his term as president of the United States. Jefferson was proud of the recognition in the scientific community which his election to the presidency of the APS represented, and he considered his election to the APS presidency, not his election to the presidency of the United States, to be the "most flattering incident" of his life. He appreciated recognition by his scientific peers at the APS because he loved the process of scientific inquiry. Jefferson respected the importance of science in the development of the nation and was proud to be a contributing member of the world community of science.

As he noted in an 1809 letter to Pierre Samuel Du Pont de Nemours, "the tranquil pursuits of science" were his "supreme delight." In 1800 he wrote happily to his daughter Martha Jefferson Randolph that he had changed his social circle in Philadelphia, "abandoning the rich . . . and associating entirely with the class of science." He viewed himself as a scientist, and he tried to apply the principles of inquiry and analysis that were used in science to all his activities, including those of a commercial, political, and social nature.

Jefferson was widely read and well informed in a range of scientific disciplines. Yet, he was not a renowned scientist in a particular discipline, as Benjamin Franklin was in the field of electricity. Franklin has been called "a scientist, indeed, a very distinguished scientist, recognized and honored the world over for his contributions to our understanding of nature and its laws." Jefferson himself paid tribute to Franklin's abilities as a scientist in *Notes on the State of Virginia:* "no one of the present age has made more important discoveries, nor has enriched philosophy with more, or more ingenious solutions of the phenomena of nature." It is particularly telling that much of Jefferson's respect for Franklin as a scientist was based on his sense that Franklin continually attempted to connect his scientific work with useful applications. In contrast, Jefferson was highly literate in a wide range of sciences, but he was not among the elite in any of those fields. Jefferson understood the ongoing work in progress in many different fields of science, and he frequently contributed to that work, but he was not a groundbreaking scientist in any particular field.

Jefferson did, however, participate in some important scientific advances of his time. For instance, he possessed a keen interest in the young field of paleontology. An avid collector and distributor of fossils, he was an active contributor to the debates in that field. His most significant involvement was with the discovery of the Megatherium (also known as the Megalonyx). In 1796 Jefferson came into possession of fossils found in western Virginia. Among these bones were those of a very large feline creature, which Jefferson named Megalonyx (meaning "giant claw"). He prepared a paper on the find for the APS. His work influenced other leading naturalists of the time, including José Garriga and Georges Cuvier. Both of those leading scientists spoke highly of Jefferson's work with fossils. Anselm Desmarest named the specimen studied by Jefferson *Megalonyx jeffersonii,* out of respect for Jefferson and his work.

Perhaps Jefferson's greatest contribution to the science of his time was his 1787 book *Notes on the State of Virginia,* which received substantial attention and praise both in America and abroad. The text covers a wide range of topics that document the natural history of Virginia. The book was written as both an examination of Virginia from a scientific perspective and a response to assessments of the American continent made by European scholars. A growing number of Americans of the time, Jefferson included, believed that many of the scientific assessments regarding America — its people, history, biology, geology, climate, and geography — made by European scholars were inaccurate and reflected an unwarranted assumption of European superiority on virtually all fronts. Jefferson's book was a response to those perceived inaccuracies and slights.

Notes on the State of Virginia also reflects Jefferson's approach to science. The publication includes substantial data collected from records and direct observation. It addresses several specific and clearly defined issues and topics. In the book Jefferson attempts to apply relevant data to resolve specific questions regarding the natural history of Virginia.

The book illustrates several of Jefferson's scientific strengths. It reveals his keen ability to make observations of natural resources and events. It highlights his meticulous attention to detail with respect to data collection and presentation. The book also underscores Jefferson's ability to present data and analysis in clear, concise written form. *Notes on the State of Virginia* offers a comprehensive and highly informative overview of the state of Virginia.

Another aspect of Jefferson's book that is worthy of note is the way it balances scientific observations with discussion of the practical implications of those observations. For example, Jefferson makes extensive observations regarding the climate of Virginia. In addition, however, he comments on the ways in which the climate affects the natural flora of the region, as well as the area's agricultural productivity. Similarly, Jefferson makes extensive observations on the geology of Virginia, and he connects those observations with some of their practical applications, such as human settlement patterns, economic development, and agricultural capabilities.

In short, *Notes on the State of Virginia* presents an outstanding sample of Jefferson's approach to science. The book offers an excellent illustration of his interest in scientific observation and analysis coupled with the practical applications of the scientific analysis. It covers a wide range of scientific disciplines and displays acute awareness of the points at which those disciplines intersect. At its best, the book combines thorough scientific observation with reasoned analysis and sensitivity to the practical implications of the scientific work.

The book also illustrates some of Jefferson's weaknesses, however. For example, the book includes racial observations and purported analyses that have no real scientific foundation, yet are presented by Jefferson as if they were fact. These inaccuracies show that Jefferson was not immune to biases and prejudices. They also suggest that he was at times willing to ignore scientific discipline and rigor in favor of advancing his own unfounded beliefs.

Jefferson and Franklin were not the only American leaders of the time who were well informed and highly active in scientific endeavors. John Adams, for one, demonstrated throughout his life an active interest in the physical and biological sciences. Adams was knowledgeable and curious about a wide range of scientific topics. That interest led him to found the American Academy of Arts and Sciences in Boston, with the intention of establishing a scientific organization similar to the APS.

Another example of the depth of scientific interest held by the first generation of American political leaders is James Madison. Jefferson's neighbor and friend, Madison also developed a keen interest in science and the potential of science to enhance the quality of life. Observers noted that Madison's interest in science was apparently cultivated and encouraged by Jefferson, and that the two friends and colleagues engaged in long communications on scientific subjects. I. Bernard Cohen describes how scientific concepts from chemistry and other fields provided effective metaphors for Madison in his *Federalist* essays. Madison's scientific reputation grew enough to lead to his election to the APS in 1785.

Another of Jefferson's political colleagues who shared an active interest in applied science was Thomas Paine. Paine's particular interest was in advocating the use of iron bridge technologies to facilitate transport and promote commerce. During the late 1700s, Paine patented his iron bridge structure in England and built a prototype. His bridge design was well received by the French Academy of Sciences. Although Paine was unable to raise adequate financing to construct the bridge, Jefferson believed that his invention had merit. Their mutual interest in technology applied to public needs gave Paine and Jefferson an additional bond beyond their shared political activism.

Jefferson's interest in science was shared by many other of his political colleagues. Shaped by Enlightenment values that promoted the search for knowledge and the application of that knowledge to improving the human condition, Jefferson's generation of political leaders was not only scientifically literate but also actively engaged in the most interesting and lively topics of scientific inquiry and discussion of their era. This knowledge and engagement made them effective and dynamic promoters of science. That close connection between government and science has not existed in America at the same level since Jefferson's time.

Jefferson lived at a time when natural events were a topic of substantial attention among intellectual leaders. Notable efforts were made by those leaders to be informed about, and when possible to participate in, the discussions and inquiries surrounding such events. The 1761 and 1769 transits of Venus, for example, attracted significant attention during Jefferson's lifetime. By observing and timing the movement of the planet Venus across the face of the sun, it was possible to calculate the radius of the earth's orbit. That calculation provided an important standard of measurement for use in making other astronomical observations and calculations. The effort to observe and measure the transit of Venus was a high point in the scientific activity of the Age of Enlightenment and attracted the attention of many of the scientific leaders of the age. As one of America's leading astronomers, David Rittenhouse played a key role. Rittenhouse's active role in the observational efforts helped to engage Jefferson's network of science peers in the enterprise.

Although subsequent political leaders have been highly supportive of science and even had technical training — Theodore Roosevelt as a naturalist, for example — we have not since the Founding Fathers had a generation of political leaders who understood and substantially influenced the process of science through direct practice. For Jefferson and his peers, knowledge of science and technology was not an extravagance or a luxury. It was, instead, an essential aspect of daily life. Jefferson and his colleagues took great joy from their involvement in the world of science.

These leaders developed and cultivated direct experience, applying principles of science and technology to their personal and professional affairs. They used their knowledge of both scientific concepts and the process of scientific inquiry when they engaged in matters of commerce and ordinary practice. They also applied that knowledge to their work in politics and government. Their literacy in fundamental scientific and technical principles meant that those principles were more than mere abstractions or theories for them. Those principles became ingrained in their approach to daily life, and they served as prominent, vigorous, and effective public ambassadors for science and technology.

Jefferson and his colleagues embraced the principles of the Enlightenment. They believed that the concepts and the mathematics developed by Newton provided the key to understanding and ultimately harnessing natural forces — including the human forces that make up society. Newton provided the means through which mankind could bring order to the natural world. There was potential, through the deliberate application of knowledge of natural forces, to influence and perhaps ultimately direct mankind's environment.

The Newtonian perspective marked a substantial shift in worldview from early times. Before, there had been the sense that natural forces were chaotic, uncontrollable influences that mankind could only endure, but Newton empowered mankind to view natural forces as actions that could be explained and understood. Based on that understanding, those forces could be controlled, harnessed for the benefit of mankind. Through his scientific work, Newton empowered mankind to play a more active role in the interaction between man and nature.

Jefferson and other political leaders influenced by Enlightenment values believed that some of the key forces that influenced human behavior could be understood and directed by application of the Newtonian models that explained many of the forces of nature. This effort to apply Newtonian principles to human activity has been characterized as part of an effort to understand "the human machinery." Newton taught us that there were mechanical models that could explain and help us to predict natural forces and actions. Jefferson and other leaders of the time endeavored to extend the Newtonian mechanical model of nature into the realm of human behavior.

Jefferson's wide-ranging scientific interests were not unusual. In many ways, Jefferson was similar to a contemporary he greatly respected, Alexander von Humboldt. Like von Humboldt's, Jefferson's scientific work is sometimes underestimated because of the range of his interests and the absence of a single breakthrough discovery or work. Both men were highly visible and effective promoters of science who made important contributions to several fields but who also had great demands placed on their time, Jefferson through his life in politics and government and von Humboldt through his extensive travels and explorations. Those intense demands limited their ability to devote full energy to science. Humboldt has been described as a "synthesizer" of science, an individual whose diverse scientific interests and experiences helped to drive several fields of science forward simultaneously. He has also been seen as "a unique commingling of the Enlightenment and the Romantic Era, of intellect and feeling, of contemplation and action." It seems reasonable to characterize Jefferson in a similar way.

Another one of these "polymaths" of the eighteenth and nineteenth centuries — men who made important contributions to various fields without being recognized as leaders in any single one — is Thomas Young, who conducted pioneering work in the study of light. A doctor, Young also made important contributions to understanding the structure and function of the human eye. He also had time to play an important role in the deciphering of the Rosetta stone.

Jefferson and the other American Founding Fathers lived during an era when polymaths thrived. They connected with each other through the knowledge networks that developed during that time. They were able to participate in the numerous advances in science and technology of the time in part because those advances were in their early stages of development. The body of knowledge in many scientific fields had not yet matured to the point where full-time focus on a specific field of work was required to reach the point of expertise and to keep abreast of continuing advances in the field. Polymaths thrived, in part, because of the immature status of science, but there was another reason as well. It was an era when rationality and reason were hailed as ideals. The pursuit of knowledge was widely embraced as an important social goal. Those who wanted to be actively engaged in the commercial, political, and social life of the time saw the study of science as the means to facilitate that engagement.

Although not among the elite scientists in any single field, Jefferson possessed several characteristics that made him a highly effective man of science across many disciplines. Jefferson was highly inquisitive. He was cautious but capable of daring insights. Perhaps most important, he had an open mind, one that was capable of altering its opinions and judgments based on new information. The astronomer Harlow Shapley noted that, collectively, these characteristics gave Jefferson an intuitive ability to engage in effective scientific analysis. Although a conservative man of science, he was always open to, and indeed often in search of, innovative insights that fundamentally altered long-held beliefs.

Jefferson was also willing to take risks based on his scientific judgments. For example, he was an early advocate of the public health value of vaccinations. Working with Dr. Benjamin Waterhouse, he played an active role in efforts to promote public acceptance of the safety and effectiveness of vaccinations. To that end, Jefferson himself was an early recipient of a smallpox vaccination, and he permitted members of his family to be vaccinated. Jefferson's willingness to take personal risks based on his scientific beliefs illustrates his commitment to research.

Jefferson had great appreciation for the importance of science to the development of society. In a 1789 letter to John Trumbull, Jefferson notes that in his estimation the three greatest men who ever lived were Francis Bacon, Isaac Newton, and John Locke. His selection of these three men is telling. They represent mankind's continuing efforts to understand and to harness the forces of nature. They were also some of the earliest advocates for reliance on rationality and reason through the application of disciplined observation, orderly experimentation, and reasoned analysis to the problems of man. Finally, they illustrate the importance of freedom and human empowerment.

Jefferson observed that scientific geniuses were of special importance to society. Writing to David Rittenhouse in 1778, he asserted that certain men of science should be encouraged to devote themselves exclusively to science, applying their unique gifts to the betterment of society. He advised Rittenhouse, whom Jefferson considered one of those geniuses, that many men can contribute to government and business, but very few possess the talents necessary to make extraordinary contributions to the advancement of science. To Jefferson, the special powers of the geniuses of science are "like air and light, the world's common property." Society should pave the way for the exceptional scientist to continue pursuit of scientific inquiry, since the results of that inquiry will prove to be beneficial for all humanity. For Jefferson, both the people who made extraordinary scientific advances and the advances themselves were part of the common heritage of mankind. They were resources that should be respected and shared by all mankind.

Jefferson held David Rittenhouse in particularly high regard. In his *Notes on Virginia,* he highlighted Rittenhouse, along with George Washington and Benjamin Franklin, as one of the leading examples of how America could produce men of genius on a par with the leading intellects of Europe. Largely self-taught, Rittenhouse developed into one of America's leading astronomers and manufacturers of scientific instruments and equipment. Jefferson admired Rittenhouse in part because of his ability to construct and operate the devices that demonstrated and applied the theories of science. Jefferson characterized Rittenhouse as "second to no astronomer living."

Rittenhouse has been described as "America's supreme mechanic," a skill that particularly impressed Jefferson. Much of Rittenhouse's international recognition as a highly skilled instrument craftsman was based on his construction of the most sophisticated version of an "orrery," a model of the universe as it was understood in the eighteenth century. Models such as the orrery were attractive to Jefferson in part because they provided mechanical representations of the forces and processes of nature. Such models made the natural world accessible to the public, and they provided a means to understand and to anticipate the processes of nature. In this way, they helped to bring order to what seemed to be a chaotic cosmos. The ability to bring a sense of order to the natural world was greatly prized by Jefferson.

Jefferson was also impressed by the independent way in which Rittenhouse achieved his stature in the scientific community. Rittenhouse essentially taught himself science through his reading and his own experiments. Jefferson valued Rittenhouse's ability to teach himself the key scientific principles of the day, and his skill at devising and implementing elegant devices that could facilitate analysis and understanding of natural forces. Some suggest that Jefferson was particularly pleased that a scientist as great as Rittenhouse could be self-taught, since it meant that the concepts identified by Newton and others were so profound and so closely tied to nature that they could be absorbed without the interference of traditional scholars from traditional academic institutions.

Jefferson's firm belief in the power of science was nurtured in his youth by several key mentors. George Wythe taught Jefferson the importance of knowledge of the classics. Francis Fauquier emphasized the value of combining scientific knowledge with humanitarian ideals. William Small led Jefferson through the world of mathematics and Newtonian analysis. Of the three, it was perhaps Small who played the greatest role in awakening an interest in mathematics and science in Jefferson as a young man. By providing him with a sound foundation in Newtonian mathematics, Small helped Jefferson become comfortable with the basic language and fundamental principles of scientific inquiry. Time and again throughout his life, Jefferson would fall back on the firm grounding in science and mathematics he developed during his youth.

William Small also provides a bridge between Jefferson and the class of businessmen in England who cultivated a strong belief in the power of science and technology to drive economic growth. After traveling there to purchase scientific equipment for the College of William and Mary, where he was teaching, Small stayed on in England. In the 1770s he was one of the founding members of a group that would become the Lunar Society of Birmingham. The Lunar Society, and other similar groups of men throughout Europe who bridged the worlds of commerce and science, played a vital role in the industrialization of the continent. Organizations like the Lunar Society and the Pneumatic Institution in Bristol, England, helped set the stage for the modern world's embrace of science and technology as critically important engines for economic development.

The Lunar Society and similar organizations in Europe and America played an important role in connecting science with a wider segment of the public. By highlighting the potential commercial applications for scientific knowledge, they helped to bridge the community of science with the world of commerce. A number of dedicated individuals who cultivated an active interest in both science and business formed networks of like-minded people, thus establishing the infrastructure that would identify and sustain many of the innovations that would drive the world to industrialization.

Jefferson appreciated the connection between scientific inquiry and a free society. Writing to Joseph Willard in 1789, Jefferson noted that "liberty is the great parent of science and virtue." He added that "a nation will be great in both in proportion as it is free." In Jefferson's estimation, "science is more important in a republican than in any other government." He saw how science and scientific inquiry provided the foundation necessary for a society to thrive and advance. Science benefited from a free society, and the society in turn benefited from the knowledge generated by the community of science. Freedom was at the heart of both a dynamic scientific community and a stable society.

It is interesting that Jefferson, a highly effective practitioner and advocate for science, played a key role in facilitating a greater level of scientific interest and literacy in the general population. He and many of his colleagues, in the United States and abroad, helped to develop a social climate in which a large segment of the population began to view science as a means to improve their economic, political, and social conditions. That climate was an important factor contributing to the development of commercial, industrialized science.

The rise of industrialized science helped societies to realize many of the economic, political, and social benefits that Jefferson and his peers anticipated and welcomed. Yet industrialized science also encouraged a less collaborative, more proprietary approach to scientific inquiry and to development of applications for the results of that inquiry. While Jefferson applauded the public benefits brought by industrialized science, he was troubled by the erosion of collaboration that also followed. Further, he did not grasp the power and importance of industrialized research as a bridge to more extensive development of commercial applications for inventions and innovations. He did not appreciate that commercial research would soon become a critical driving force for technological advances.

JEFFERSON THE INVENTOR

Jefferson highly prized the skills of the inventor and the innovator, especially those individuals who applied their knowledge and creativity in pursuit of advances with a positive impact on daily life. In a 1787 letter to Jeudy de l'Hommande, Jefferson noted that "every discovery which multiplies the subsistence of men must be a matter of joy to every friend of humanity."

Jefferson made a similar point in a 1794 letter to Richard Morris commenting on the invention of waterproof cloth. Jefferson observed that the invention had particular merit and promise because it had the potential to make waterproof material available at low enough cost to enable the general public to make use of the advance. The waterproofing capability was innovative and useful, but what made it particularly attractive to Jefferson was its potential to bring the benefits associated with waterproofing to the masses.

For Jefferson, the true value of an innovation was its usefulness in daily life. Inventions should serve the public, making their lives more comfortable and productive, and the knowledge generated by science provided the foundation necessary to enable such inventions. Jefferson saw inventors as the connection between the knowledge generated by science and the beneficial social impact he perceived as the ultimate goal of science. Science established human understanding of nature; inventors applied that knowledge for the benefit of the public.

All advances in knowledge and understanding were of value, but Jefferson placed greatest emphasis on those advances that could be transformed into practical benefits for people most in need. This is an important aspect of his philosophy regarding intellectual property. He favored encouraging widespread participation in the knowledge networks of his time. He believed that as those networks grew, the collection of public knowledge would also grow. If those knowledge networks remained open and active, their knowledge would be more readily transformed into practical applications that would work to the benefit of the general public.

Jefferson's inquisitive nature and his focus on practical applications made him an active mechanical tinkerer. His skills were particularly well suited to refining machines and devices for more efficient operations and more diverse uses. Jefferson was an inventor, but he was interested more in improving existing products than in creating new ones. His work as an inventor focused on agricultural equipment, like the plow, and labor-saving devices, like the polygraph. He also worked with a device known as the cipher wheel, a cryptographic instrument that made use of concentric wheels to code and decode messages. Jefferson developed a prototype of the device and experimented with it while on diplomatic missions, but he never sought to commercialize it.

An active writer, Jefferson was interested in technologies that facilitated the process of writing. For example, he greatly appreciated the convenience and value offered by the polygraph, a device that enabled a writer to make multiple copies of a document at the same time. He actively used the polygraph and promoted its utility to his many friends and colleagues.

Jefferson also paid substantial attention to improving the effectiveness of the plow. In particular, he conducted extensive work on the moldboard component of plows. As a farmer, Jefferson had a personal interest in improving plows and other agricultural equipment. It is interesting to note, however, that despite his active interest in agricultural technology, Jefferson was not an adept or successful farmer.

Historians have devoted significant attention to Jefferson's innovative work on plow moldboard design. While the coulter of a plow cuts through soil, the primary function of the wedge-shaped moldboard is to raise the soil and turn it. Jefferson's work on moldboard design was an attempt to devise a wedge shape for the moldboard that would offer the least resistance as it moved through the soil. It has been noted that a critical portion of Jefferson's efforts to complete this design involved use of the mathematics devised by Isaac Newton. Some observers link Jefferson's moldboard design efforts with examples presented in Newton's *Principia,* where Newton applied his mathematics to the challenge of identifying shapes for solids that minimized the resistance offered by those objects.

Jefferson did not patent any of the advances he developed for the moldboard. He elected not to treat those innovations as proprietary material but worked to make his work widely accessible. He wanted farmers everywhere to have access to the benefits resulting from his work. Instead of seeking patent rights, Jefferson published his results, presenting the moldboard modifications to the APS in 1798. His actions highlight the emphasis Jefferson placed on the dissemination of knowledge and operational advances. Jefferson considered his innovations to be contributions to the art, and it was his intent that they be rapidly put into practice. Instead of pursuing intellectual property rights for his work,

Jefferson chose to disclose it publicly through the nation's leading scientific society.

Jefferson's work with moldboard design also underscores his interest in applying abstract concepts to practical applications and illustrates the extent of his interest in, and facility with, mathematics. Jefferson took virtually every opportunity to quantify the challenges of daily life and to apply mathematics to resolve those challenges. He was comfortable with numbers and trained in mathematics. For him, mathematics provided a fundamental analytical tool that could be applied in every facet of human endeavor.

Jefferson's interest in the application of scientific, mathematical, and technical principles and concepts to real world challenges and needs is also reflected in his passion for architecture. Few fields bridge the worlds of theory and practice as comprehensively as architecture. Jefferson's lifelong and passionate interest in architecture developed not because of cultural influences but because he wanted to be directly involved in construction. He was a builder, and he derived great pleasure from both the planning and the execution of structural construction. Whether working on his beloved Monticello, the structures that would become the University of Virginia, or any of the many other construction projects with which he would be associated during his lifetime, Jefferson maintained an energetic interest in both the theory and the practice of architectural design.

Jefferson could be extremely generous in his praise and support for inventions he believed to be particularly useful. For example, in his 1798 letter to John Taylor discussing Thomas Martin's hand threshing machine, Jefferson described Martin's improvements as "beautiful" and characterized the device as "the most compleat machine in the world for sowing a single row." A true inventor, Jefferson could never stop seeking improvements on devices, and so after praising the quality of Martin's machine, Jefferson offered his own set of additional modifications, which he viewed as enhancements to the device. The process of innovation was, for Jefferson, relentless and unending. No creation was perfect. All could benefit from the efforts of others to refine and enhance their utility. Instead of rushing to patent each new innovation upon completion, Jefferson preferred to get immediately back to work searching for ways to make the invention more effective and more widely useful.

He was often supportive and encouraging in his interaction with inventors. In an 1807 letter to Robert Fulton, Jefferson expressed full confidence that the submarine and torpedo technology Fulton was pioneering would one day constitute an important part of American defense. Even when he was unconvinced that a proposed device could, in fact, accomplish its stated purpose, Jefferson nonetheless encouraged additional experimentation. In a 1797 letter to John Oliver regarding an invention developed by Oliver's son, he exhorted the inventor to make the invention's "performance so certain as to prove itself by action and leave nothing to hypothesis."

Jefferson possessed the daring of an innovator. He was willing to risk failure in pursuit of improvements. This acceptance of uncertainty and risk is a key aspect of the psychology of innovation. As Jefferson wrote to Robert Fulton in 1810, "I am not afraid of new inventions or improvements." Yet he also insisted that inventions should have a foundation in existing knowledge. In his letter to Fulton he added that "where a new invention is supported by well-known principles, and promises to be useful, it ought to be tried." This stance reflects his balance between daring scientific inquiry and insistence on a rational basis for the calculated risk. Jefferson was not a radically creative inventor. He preferred to work to address specific needs through focused, incremental improvements based on recognized principles of science and mathematics.

Perhaps Jefferson's continuing focus on refining and enhancing existing products and processes, rather than developing entirely novel devices, is a reflection of the emphasis he placed on the utility of inventions. He was eager to make innovations more widely available and ever more useful. Work involving refinements for existing equipment is more likely to yield success than is more speculative work. To the extent that the work generates successful advances, those advances are more likely to be put to use more quickly when they are associated with already existing products.

In addition, Jefferson placed great emphasis on the ability to document effects. It is often easier to document and assess the performance impact of product improvements than it is to evaluate the impact of new devices that perform a previously unperformed function. Refinements to an existing device can always be evaluated based on the performance of the modified version relative to that of the original, which provides a baseline performance standard. In addition, feedback from users of the original device provides a basis for enhancements to improve performance of the original function or to allow the device to perform new ones.

Jefferson's devotion to finding improvements and refinements in existing products may also be connected to the fact that he was an active consumer of a great many of the products of his time. As an active farmer, architect, and builder, Jefferson was continually in search of devices that could improve quality, enhance productivity, and reduce cost. That search involved incessant monitoring of the most recent technological advances, as well as perpetual tinkering with existing technology in an effort to make it better suited to meet his needs as a user. In part, Jefferson's work as an inventor refining and enhancing a diverse range of existing products was an effort to customize those products to make them more suitable for his own use. Because he was largely motivated by his own needs as a consumer of technology, he was particularly in tune with the demands of technology users in general.

Jefferson was curious about a wide range of innovative devices appropriate for a diverse variety of applications. For example, as noted above, he was intrigued by a cryptographic device known as a "wheel cipher." Jefferson appreciated the value of a convenient yet effective device for encrypting and decrypting messages for use in official government communications, particularly those executed outside the United States. He developed and tested a prototype of a wheel cipher that made use of concentric rings to code and decode messages. The cipher wheel was based on previous work by several inventors, and Jefferson worked to refine those efforts. He never pursued commercial development of his version of the device. Jefferson's work with the cipher wheel illustrates several characteristics of his style as an inventor. It underscores the wide range of Jefferson's interests, and it shows his desire to focus on inventions that have close connections with practical uses and needs. His work with the cipher wheel also highlights Jefferson's general lack of interest in commercialization of his inventive efforts. Additionally, the project is an example of Jefferson's willingness to study and build on the work of others.

Although Jefferson was a strong advocate for, and sympathetic adviser to, inventors, he could also be a demanding critic if their work fell short of his high standards. For Jefferson, the greatest inventors were those who created unique, truly novel advances that could be readily applied to practical applications for the good of mankind. As a practical matter, however, he recognized that truly novel works of invention and creation are extremely rare. Far more common are modifications and changes to existing devices and processes, and Jefferson appreciated the value to the public of these improvements. Thus while he appreciated the brilliance of those who could devise truly novel works, he placed greater emphasis on the ability to apply inventiveness to increase productivity and to meet additional human needs. For Jefferson, utility of inventions was of greater significance than their novelty.

At least in part, Jefferson's appreciation for incremental advances may be attributable to his extensive involvement in the world's scientific community. That experience led him to understand that true moments of discovery and independent insight are rare. Far more often, the advances made by one individual build upon the work and insights of many others who came before. Scientific advances evolve over time, as individual scientists share their knowledge and each contributes additional insights based on the work of all predecessors.

With such a perspective it is not surprising that Jefferson was most critical of those who, in his judgment, overstated the novelty of their scientific and technological work. He could be quite harsh to those who failed to acknowledge the prior work upon which their findings were based. In his estimation, the vast majority of inventions were derivative in some way of prior work conducted by many others. For Jefferson, there was substantial potential value to the public in such derivative work, but he objected to those who refused to recognize the prior work of others and who overestimated the novelty of their own efforts. An example of an inventor who drew this type of critical reaction from Jefferson was Jacob Isaacks.

THE CASE OF JACOB ISAACKS

In the 1700s one of the major challenges facing navies and commercial fleets was the ability to provide enough fresh water for drinking to sustain ship crews through long voyages. The ability to carry or otherwise access adequate drinking water was one of the key limiting factors to the length and direction of sea voyages. The simplest conceptual answer to this challenge was desalination of seawater. If an effective and economical desalination process could be developed, sea crews could, theoretically, have access to all the drinking water they required for even the longest of voyages. Not surprisingly, all seafaring nations experimented with desalination systems that would be effective and reliable, yet also readily transportable and economical.

In the late 1700s Jacob Isaacks claimed to have resolved the challenge of creating an effective shipboard desalination system. He contended that his system made use of an innovative wood-burning distillation process that enabled more refined temperature control. He approached the U.S. Congress offering to sell the system to the U.S. Navy. In 1791 Congress asked Jefferson to evaluate the merits of the Isaacks system and to recommend a course of action. Jefferson approached the project in a way consistent with his analytical style. He convened a panel of experts to examine the system, and he asked Isaacks to provide a demonstration of the system to the panel.

Jefferson called on two of his scientific colleagues, David Rittenhouse and Caspar Wistar, to serve with him on the review panel. Jefferson's decision to enlist two of the scientists he most admired illustrates the seriousness with which he treated the review. It suggests the respect Jefferson afforded his fellow inventor Isaacks, offering him the courtesy of a thorough review providing for differing opinions on the merits of the proposal. It also provides a clear example of Jefferson's willingness to seek input from professionals whose judgment he respected.

On March 21, 1791, Jacob Isaacks demonstrated his desalination system to the panel. Isaacks's system used a wood-burning fire to distill seawater into drinkable water. Wood-fired distillation was not a new idea, and many similar systems had been tried in the past. Isaacks contended, however, that his system was different and better than the others. By using a proprietary mixture of different types of wood, Isaacks claimed, his distillation process was more efficient than all previous systems.

The panel spent more than a day questioning Isaacks. In addition, they required Isaacks to conduct multiple test runs using different wood combinations. The demonstration and interrogation were extensive as the panel probed Isaacks and his invention.

The panel concluded that the Isaacks desalination system provided an effective approach to desalination. However, the panel also concluded that Isaacks's system was not the only effective desalination system then available. The panel noted that several effective systems had been developed over the years. Isaacks work was thus effective but not unique, and the panel could not determine which desalination system would be best for use by the navy.

Jefferson and his colleagues recommended that information regarding the Isaacks system be made available to the navy and to commercial fleets. Based on that disclosure, fleets or individual vessels could experiment with the Isaacks system and compare it with other approaches to desalination. The panel did not recommend that Congress purchase the Isaacks system. Instead, it advocated public disclosure without compensation to Isaacks.

Not surprisingly, Isaacks was not pleased with the recommendation made by Jefferson and his colleagues. In Isaacks's eyes, Jefferson was recommending public disclosure of information that he considered to be proprietary. Isaacks had intended to exploit his system commercially by selling it to the U.S. government. Instead, he was faced with the prospect that his intellectual property was to be placed into the public domain, with no compensation to him.

Jefferson viewed the situation far differently. To him, Isaacks's system was an interesting and potentially useful modification made to work that had been conducted by many other people in different countries over the years. It was not clear that Isaacks's system was a substantial improvement over the others. The best way to determine its utility was to put it into use under realistic conditions, and the most effective way to get those field trials under way was to publish the details of the system so that interested parties could try it.

Isaacks was certainly free to promote and to participate in such trials. He was free to charge for services and equipment associated with use of the desalination system. For Jefferson, Isaacks's potential commercial reward lay in his ability to promote the system and to build a business around selling equipment and services associated with it. Jefferson did not view the modifications to prior work made by Isaacks to be of the sort that should be treated as intellectual property.

Jefferson's approach to the desalination system of Jacob Isaacks provides insight into his views on inventors and the process of invention. When asked to evaluate the new system, Jefferson invited input from highly regarded technical experts, Rittenhouse and Wistar. Jefferson based his evaluation on an extensive review of prior art and on a rigorous, interactive demonstration of the system. The focus of his review was on whether the system provided an improvement over existing approaches to the desalination challenge and whether the system was truly novel in nature. In effect, the review he provided was similar to the type of evaluation Jefferson commonly led when reviewing patent applications (see chapter 5).

Jefferson did not merely investigate to see whether the Isaacks system would provide an economical and effective desalination process. Instead he saw it as his mission to take the inquiry an additional step to determine whether the system provided the best available desalination system. Jefferson and the panel concluded that the Isaacks system was likely to be effective, but they could not determine whether it was the most effective or the most economical system available.

Although Jefferson harbored profound respect for inventors,

that respect was largely based on their ability to provide devices and processes with applications that were useful to the general population. An inventor who independently created a truly unique device or method was entitled to a patent, thus establishing proprietary control over the invention. Jefferson knew, however, that that type of invention was rare. Far more common was the situation that Jacob Isaacks found himself in, where the inventor has built upon the knowledge and creativity of others working in the same field. While Jefferson recognized the value of these incremental modifications and advances, he was reluctant to treat such incremental work as proprietary. The most important objective was disclosure of those modifications and advances so that they could be tested, compared with other work, and used as the basis for additional enhancements and improvements.

Also worth noting is Jefferson's recognition that Isaacks was clearly entitled to attempt to persuade the owners and operators of seagoing vessels to use his desalination system instead of another system. He assumed that Isaacks would be able to benefit commercially by offering the equipment and services necessary to support his desalination process. Jefferson did not deny Isaacks's ability to derive commercial gain from his system, but he was not willing to provide the means for him to limit the availability of alternative desalination systems.

In fact, Jefferson preferred that several different desalination systems be made available for use. That approach would create a competitive environment in which the different systems could be tested and compared. He was confident that the competition would lead to improvements in the various systems and widespread acceptance of the most effective and useful ones. This approach is perfectly sensible from the perspective of society as a whole, but it displays an essentially complete lack of sympathy for the strategy of proprietary commercialization of intellectual property. Proprietary commercialization relies upon some period of exclusivity, whether that period is the result of a patent or of skill on the part of the commercializing party. As the encounter with Isaacks suggests, Jefferson was philosophically reluctant to encouraging exclusivity with respect to innovations.

Jefferson's interaction with Isaacks shows that he placed the greatest priority on the effectiveness of any invention. The only way to assess that effectiveness is to test the invention rigorously. That testing requires review and input from as many informed sources as possible. It also requires actual use of the invention. Jefferson found any efforts to reduce the level of testing to be unacceptable.

His approach to the desalination system also illustrates Jefferson's emphasis on the value of continuing improvements for devices. Disclosure of information regarding an invention and promotion of multiple systems to perform a function foster a climate of continuing refinement and improvement for inventions. Jefferson's proposal for the Isaacks desalination system provided an effective environment for finding continued enhancements for the system.

This perspective would virtually always place Jefferson at odds with a patent applicant or a patentee. Unless an inventor could clearly demonstrate novelty, Jefferson would be reluctant to provide the exclusivity that a patent offers. Instead, Jefferson would encourage commercialization of all available technologies, viewing the resulting competition as operational testing of the different approaches. The result is likely consistent with the public interest, but will almost always be disappointing to the inventors. Although he harbored great respect for inventors, and he recognized the vital service they performed for society, Jefferson refused to place their interests above those of the public. He apparently believed that the process of invention would continue effectively even with minimal use of the encouragement and incentives that exclusive commercialization opportunities provide to inventors.

Jefferson's approach to the commercialization of technology placed greatest emphasis on an inventor's ability to compete effectively on the merits of his invention. Priority of invention provided a competitive advantage, but not an insurmountable one. The developer of an improved version of a device could succeed commercially. To Jefferson, the key to commercial success should be the effectiveness and utility of the invention. Jefferson displayed no appreciation for the economic demands associated with commercial research and development.

Jefferson also argued, in effect, for open standards for technology. With regard to desalination systems, he advocated publication of information regarding all viable systems. By making that information readily accessible, different parties could design their systems to be compatible with other technologies in service. There would most likely be available, not a single dominant technology or system, but instead a variety of technologies. In that situation, there would be commercial advantage to those systems that were interoperable with each other.

Issues associated with the interoperability of technology from different sources continue to be an important challenge today. Much attention is now directed to the benefits that result when technologies offered by different providers can interconnect seamlessly and function together without difficulty. Without such open systems, it is possible for the first technology provider that reaches the marketplace to establish technical standards that can place it at an unfair competitive advantage. That situation may be ideal for the first provider, but it is not ideal for users of the technology or for future innovation. Jefferson seems to have recognized the broader public benefits associated with the cultivation of competition among providers of an emerging technology.

AN AMBASSADOR FOR SCIENCE AND INVENTION

Jefferson's range of interests and expertise made him a good friend of the community of scientists and inventors. He admired their creativity and their ability to improve the human condition. Dumas Malone provided a particularly apt description of Jefferson's relationship with science and invention, noting that people in many different parts of the world knew that Jefferson was "interested in all varieties of learning, in every form of inquiry into Nature and its laws, in every invention that might contribute to human comfort and well-being."

Yet he was not willing to permit scientists or inventors to restrict acquisition of additional knowledge or to limit future applications for their work. Jefferson fit comfortably in the community of scientists accustomed to a communal approach to research and advancement. His approach was also compatible with the line of inventors who focused on rapid diffusion of their work into practical applications. But Jefferson was not comfortable with the line of inventors, just beginning to come to prominence in his time, who emphasized proprietary rights as a means for personal gain.

Jefferson appreciated the ways in which communities of scientists and inventors contributed to society and saw those communities as key components of a successful democracy. In addition, he viewed the communities of scientists and inventors as open and egalitarian groups, in which both ideas and individuals rose and fell based on their merits.

Jefferson was also an active and able representative of the community of scientists and inventors to the public at large. His passion for scientific inquiry and his perpetual interest in invention and innovation were readily apparent in his actions as a political leader. Jefferson sought to apply the principles of science and the scientific method of investigation and invention to all aspects of society, and in so doing he acted as an exceptional emissary on behalf of the world of science and invention.

Jefferson's experience provided him with a wealth of understanding of the processes through which science is conducted. He also learned, from direct experience, the methods through which the fruits of science led to the development of technology, which could in turn be applied to meet human needs. Jefferson had years of experience as a developer, distributor, and user of intellectual property. He was an intellectual property practitioner, and his notions of intellectual property rights were shaped by that practical background.

FOUR

THE FIRST
PATENT
EXAMINER

When Jefferson assumed his position on the first Board of Arts for the United States, he moved from the realm of scientist inventor to that of patent examiner. Previously, Jefferson had been a developer and user of intellectual property. Once on the board, he became a patent official. Figuratively speaking, he jumped the fence in the world of intellectual property rights. Clearly, he retained his ideals regarding the importance of knowledge sharing and access to inventive works; however, his role and perspective on intellectual property rights shifted. As a member of the Board of Arts, it was now his duty to place into operation and to manage a bureaucratic system to review patent applications. From his position on the board, Jefferson would see another side of the world of intellectual property practice.

The Patent Act of 1790 established the American process for obtaining patent rights. The concept of intellectual property rights protection is rooted in the U.S. Constitution. Article I, Section 8, of the Constitution expressly provides for legal protection for the useful arts. It empowers Congress to "promote progress of science and the useful arts by securing for limited times to authors and inventors the exclusive right to their respective writings and discoveries." This provision is the foundation for both patent and copyright law in the United States. The presence of this clause in the Constitution underscores the significance placed on the concept of intellectual property by the early leaders of our nation.

One of the leading proponents of addressing intellectual property rights in the Constitution was C. C. Pinckney, of South Carolina. Before ratification of the Constitution, the states themselves addressed intellectual property rights issues, and thanks to the attention of Pinckney, South Carolina was one of the more active states in this area. With support from James Madison, Pinckney was able to persuade his colleagues to include a provision establishing intellectual property rights as part of the scope of the national government's authority.

I. Bernard Cohen addresses the issue of the connection between promoting the progress of science and the useful arts and granting exclusive rights to authors and inventors. For Cohen, these are expressions of two separate aspects of science and technology policy. The Constitution reflects an Enlightenment sensibility regarding the importance of science. It also recognizes value in empowering creators of new works. The Constitution does not necessarily, however, equate the grant of exclusive rights to authors and inventors with the effective promotion of science and the useful arts. It seems that the founders of this nation appreciated both the importance of government promotion of science and respect for the rights of authors and inventors, yet they did not necessarily directly connect the two concepts. They did not assume that grant of exclusive rights to authors and inventions would necessarily promote science and the useful arts. As we see today, there are indeed many instances in which exclusive rights for authors and inventors may in fact impede the continuing development of science and the useful arts.

The distinction drawn by Cohen is an important one. The Founding Fathers did not confine their interest in promoting science and development of the useful arts to the grant of rights to inventors and authors. They did not assume that the grant of such rights was either necessary or sufficient to promote continuing advances in science and technological applications. Management of intellectual property rights was not to be the sole focus of government with respect to the promotion of progress in science and technology. Jefferson and his colleagues did not assume that grant of exclusive rights to authors and inventors would necessarily provide adequate promotion in support of progress in science and the useful arts. This is an important lesson for us today.

Although the Constitution reflects recognition of the value that the grant of exclusive rights to the creators of new works offers for society, it does not assume that grant of those rights alone will provide effective support for progress in science and the useful arts. It is not reasonable to conclude that our founders believed that exclusive rights for authors and inventors would be adequate to promote progress in science and the application of science. It is also a mistake for us to assume, today, that emphasis on the rights of the creators of original works will be sufficient to promote and facilitate progress.

Appreciation for the distinction between promotion of science and the useful arts and the award of exclusive rights to authors and inventors is particularly important today. Much of our current debate on intellectual property rights policy focuses on the rights of creators. It is particularly important, in such a climate, to recognize that those who established the constitutional basis for intellectual property rights also acknowledged the importance of promoting science and innovation, and that they did not necessarily believe that granting exclusive rights to authors and inventors would satisfy the goal of promoting science and its useful applications. The Founding Fathers apparently saw that there were two distinct objectives involved, and they did not favor one over the other.

Cohen also recognizes that Jefferson and his colleagues certainly appreciated the distinction between what we characterize today as basic and applied science. They understood that inquiry into the structure and operation of natural forces, of the sort conducted by Newton and others, constituted a form of science more distant from practical applications than the work of inventors and engineers. Cohen suggests that the political leaders of the time were nonetheless aware that even basic research held the potential for dramatic practical use, since they were well aware of the impact of Franklin's experiments with the lightning rod. Franklin conducted fundamental inquires into the nature of electricity, and based on that research he developed the lightning rod. The lightning rod proved to be a useful device, and its existence evolved from pure scientific research aimed at increasing fundamental knowledge.

The Founding Fathers thus recognized the distinction between basic and applied science; they further appreciated that basic science forms the foundation for applied science. All useful applications for science grow from basic research. Understanding this connection between basic and applied science reflects a sophisticated awareness of the process of scientific discovery and the application of scientific knowledge. Both basic and applied science were necessary to secure the progress that the founders of our nation envisioned.

The 1790 act provided a process to execute the constitutional patent mandate. Under the act, anyone who "invented or discovered any useful art, manufacture, engine, machine or device, or any improvement therein, not before known or used" could petition the government for a patent. The patent petitions were to be submitted to the secretary of state and reviewed by the Board of Arts. The 1790 act did not provide extensive direction as to the mechanics of the patent application and approval process. Many of the operational details of the fledgling U.S. patent system were developed through the practical decisions made by the first Board of Arts.

While secretary of state, Jefferson served as one of the three founding members of the Board of Arts. In that capacity, he and his colleagues, the secretary of war and the attorney general, reviewed and acted upon all patent applications submitted in the United States. Jefferson's colleagues on that first Board of Arts were Henry Knox and Edmund Randolph. In effect, the Board of Arts functioned as the first American patent examiners. Based on their review and assessment of described inventions, patents were either issued or denied. No other American president has had such a direct involvement in the daily operations of the patent process of the United States. In this chapter, we assess Jefferson's role as the first practicing patent official in the United States and consider what that experience suggests regarding Jefferson's perception of intellectual property rights.

The U.S. Patent Act of 1790 established patent rights for useful art, manufacture, engines, machines, devices, and their improvements. The Patent Act established the Board of Arts as the government body tasked with consideration of patent requests. Any American inventor could petition the Board of Arts, requesting a patent for his work. The act did not specify the application procedures required for consideration, so the task of specifying the material necessary for a patent petition fell to Jefferson and his colleagues on the first Board of Arts. The process that was ultimately established required petitions to the Board of Arts including sworn or affirmed evidence that the invention in question was the work of the petitioner. The petitions were also to include associated descriptions, drawings, specimens, and working models for the invention. Based on the petitions and associated documentation, the Board of Arts made its decision regarding grant of patent protection.

American patent law had its origins in the European legal concept of government-issued monopolies. From medieval times, the sovereign had the right to grant monopolies for products and services. Those monopoly grants provided a means to facilitate the introduction of new offerings and to raise funds for the state. From as early as the fifteenth century, some of those monopolies were applied to inventions. Patents were government-provided monopoly rights intended to facilitate the introduction of new products, both those that were original creations and those that were in use in other countries but new to the country granting the patent.

In England, movement toward placing some limitations on the range of monopoly grants developed during the seventeenth century. The first limitation was a restriction requiring that monopolies be issued only for goods that were new to England, thus using the monopoly grant as a means of facilitating the availability of new products for the English public. In 1624 the English Parliament acted to restrict the duration of crown monopoly grants. The Statute of Monopolies placed a finite term (fourteen years) on the duration of crown monopolies. It also limited the topics for which patent grants could be awarded. The statute essentially limited patent grants to inventions that were new to the English marketplace and that would be useful to the public. Patents could be obtained for inventions that were entirely novel and for inventions that were merely new to the English market.

The English approach to patents emphasized value to the society. Patents were intended to provide incentive and opportunity for new and useful products to be made available to the citizens of England. The system was not designed as a reward for the work of inventors. Instead, the commercial opportunity afforded by patents was viewed as an incentive for behavior that would serve the broader public interest.

The English patent system was cumbersome for the patentee. The high cost and administrative burden associated with the system had a notable impact on its effectiveness. They made the English system more accessible to affluent inventors and those supported by financially strong patrons, but discouraged the individual inventor. It required substantial resources to obtain and to maintain patents, resources commonly beyond the means of the average individual.

Other nations had different ways of treating patents. For instance, in 1791 the French adopted a patent system that was based simply on registration. A patent applicant was required to describe the invention in a such a manner that a person reasonably skilled in the relevant art could replicate it. There was no requirement to demonstrate its effectiveness, nor was there a requirement to show that the invention was novel. Grant of the patent did not constitute any form of government evaluation of the merits of the invention. When the patent was issued, however, the patentee would have a period of two years to put the invention into practice. If the invention was not in use at the end of the two-year period, and if there was no mitigating explanation for the delay in commercialization, the patent could be revoked.

It is worth noting that the French made use of other government initiatives, in addition to the patent process, to encourage invention and innovation. For example, French law of the time gave inventors the option of donating their invention to the nation in exchange for an award of funds supplied by the government. This option was only available to inventors who could demonstrate that their invention had substantial public value. The government of France also awarded medals and other prizes to inventors who successfully met specific technical challenges devised by the government.

France was not the only nation to make use of these technology-inducing competitions. For example, the English government sponsored a heated and protracted competition to devise a method of tracking longitude for navigation. France also provided other incentives to the most effective inventors by granting them pensions and other forms of financial support. Under certain circumstances the French government would also purchase patent rights associated with particularly useful inventions. After purchase, the government would release those inventions into the public domain. In the eighteenth and nineteenth century the French government applied a more diverse range of incentives to encourage invention and innovation than did either the English or the American governments.

The French approach to patents also placed greater emphasis on the rights of the inventor than did the English system. While the English system focused almost entirely on an assessment of the anticipated public benefit associated with the invention, the French system recognized inventions as the fruits of creative labor and the property of their inventors. This viewpoint set the stage for French inventors to assert property claims in their work that stood outside the patent grant.

Colonial America was integrated into the English system of patents. Some of the earliest patents issued in America were granted by the crown in the Massachusetts Bay Colony. After the revolution and during the period of American confederacy, each state developed its own system of patents. When the U.S. federal government began to coalesce, patent law came under the control of the national government. Jefferson's friend and colleague James Madison played a role in that nationalization by facilitating inclusion of the intellectual property powers in the Constitution. But the Constitution and the first U.S. national patent legislation provided little practical guidance for the first American patent office.

Largely because of Jefferson's experience as a scientist and inventor, he played an active role on the Board of Arts. Deeply interested in a wide range of technologies and technical topics, Jefferson effectively functioned as the leader of the Board of Arts while he served on it. He exercised that leadership by taking the most active role in reviewing, testing, and considering the various petitions for patents presented to the board. A man who enjoyed tinkering with new technologies and working to develop solutions to technical challenges, Jefferson was in many ways very well suited to play the role of patent examiner, and he was diligent about examining the material submitted by applicants.

As a patent examiner, Jefferson placed substantial emphasis on certain key criteria. He insisted that inventions have useful functions and that they be capable of effectively executing those functions. This patent law criterion is known as "utility." Only if an invention is able to complete a useful task does it merit patent protection. The concept of utility does not require that an invention always be successful at performing its defined function. Instead, the principle of utility requires that an invention have a specific and clearly definable function, and that it can be demonstrated that the invention is, in fact, capable of performing that defined function.

In addition to the utility requirement, Jefferson emphasized the concept of "novelty" when reviewing patent applications. Novelty, for patent law purposes, involves essentially the principle of uniqueness. When considering a patent application, we assess the extent to which the invention represents an advance beyond existing knowledge, the current "prior art." Patents are awarded for those inventions that represent notable extensions beyond current knowledge. Jefferson placed great significance on the requirement of novelty. He did not want to reward less innovative work through the grant of patent protection.

The patent law principle of novelty differs from the principle of originality that is at the heart of copyright law. Copyright law protects the expression of original works fixed in tangible form. Originality for copyright law purposes means simply that the work was created by the author, independent of the works of others. If the work is original to the author, it can be protected by copyright, even if another author created an identical or substantially similar work. If there has been no copying, a work is deemed to be original and is eligible for copyright protection.

The concept of novelty under patent law today is more rigorous than copyright law's notion of originality. Novelty equates to uniqueness. To qualify as a novel work, an invention must be different than all other works that have been patented or otherwise disclosed. This means that if an identical or substantially similar invention has been described, used, or distributed prior to the creation of the invention, the invention will not be patentable. This barrier to subsequent patenting exists even if the second inventor was not aware of the prior invention.

It is important to recognize that the emphasis Jefferson placed on novelty in the patent process did not mean that he did not appreciate the value of work that was not novel, but was useful. As discussed previously, Jefferson had great respect for the value of incremental improvements in devices. To the extent that those improvements could make a device more useful or more broadly applicable, Jefferson believed that the improvements were of great value. For patent purposes, however, he believed that only truly novel inventions should be awarded patent protection. For Jefferson, work that might not be patentable could surely still be highly valuable. He did not correlate patentability with economic or social value.

Jefferson's appreciation of the value of refinements and enhancements made to existing work reflects his understanding of the way that products actually evolve. Virtually no product springs into existence as a totally novel creation. The vast majority represent modifications and refinements made to prior work. Once a product emerges into use, the work of refining and modifying it continues. It is always possible to make a device better, and to find new applications for it. Only after a product has been put into use can its merits and weaknesses be identified. For Jefferson, the refinements and new applications that develop from the feedback of users all added more value to the original product and made the invention truly useful. They were an essential part of the process of invention.

Jefferson's pursuit of novelty was limited geographically. The early American patent system did not bar the patenting of inventions that had been developed and patented by others in other countries. In the beginning the U.S. patent system did not formally include patents in other countries or prior use of an invention in those countries as part of the prior art. The patent system in the United States, and for that matter in England and France as well, placed greatest emphasis on rapid introduction of new, useful products into the home marketplace. The fact that an invention was already patented or widely used in another country did not prevent its patenting in America. The roots of patent law, the early crown patent grants, specifically sought to encourage introduction of inventions from other countries by allowing parties other than the foreign patentees to obtain patents. Clearly, this objective of early patent law was at odds with the concept of requiring novelty for patent protection.

Note that Jefferson's focus on utility and novelty was not specifically required by either the Constitution or the 1790 Patent Act. Instead, it was an outgrowth of his efforts to execute the more general provisions on patenting provided by the Constitution and the 1790 act. The Constitution and the act envisioned patent protection for advances in the useful arts. For Jefferson, evaluation of an invention's contribution to the useful arts required an assessment of the usefulness of the invention (utility) and an evaluation of the extent to which the invention extended the scope of knowledge in the field (novelty). Only those creations that had a useful purpose and offered new solutions to practical concerns merited patent protection. His insistence on utility and novelty were consistent with his desire to limit the scope of patenting to those instances when the invention offered clear value to the public. Inventions that could satisfy the utility and novelty criteria were more likely to offer new benefits to the society, and were thus worthy of the monopoly rights that Jefferson sought to grant as sparingly as possible.

Modern patent law also imposes a requirement that inventions be nonobvious to one who is reasonably well schooled in the art most directly relevant to the invention. This requirement of nonobviousness was not present in Jefferson's time. It attempts to prevent the award of patents for work that, although technically new, does not represent unexpected advance over the current art. The notion behind the requirement of nonobviousness is that the advance may not have been patented before because it was so widely anticipated that no one considered it to be a notable advance in the art.

Although Jefferson did not speak to or develop the concept of nonobviousness, it is a principle that addresses some of the concerns that troubled him. Since Jefferson was concerned about the monopoly aspect of patent rights, he consistently looked for ways to limit the scope of patenting. His method of limiting patent reach was to emphasize the requirements of utility and novelty. The nonobviousness requirement adds another criterion that serves to limit patenting, and is one that would likely have appealed to Jefferson. Jefferson saw patents as appropriate and effective rewards for inventors, but he sought to limit those rewards to the instances when the work involved was most useful and innovative. The concept of nonobviousness helps to ensure that patents are provided only to the more innovative work.

It is difficult, however, to evaluate the extent to which an invention is or is not obvious, given the state of the prior art in its field. The standard of nonobviousness is highly subjective. In the present day we have substantial difficulty applying the standard as patent applications are assessed. Although it is rare for the U.S. Supreme Court to examine patent law issues, the Court did so in its 2007 decision in the case *KSR International v. Teleflex, Inc.* A key issue in that case was interpretation of the patent law standard of nonobviousness. The Court concluded that nonobviousness cannot be subjected to a formal, rigid standard. Instead, each court must be willing to examine the evidence before it and make a case-by-case determination of whether the specific facts associated with a given invention support a finding of nonobviousness.

Although the ruling provides little firm guidance on the assessment of nonobviousness, the case is significant in that the Court's willingness to rule on this patent matter illustrates its recognition of the significance of patent enforcement matters. As to the impact of the ruling, it seems likely that it will assist defendants in patent infringement cases by making it easier for them to introduce evidence that the invention at issue did not meet the nonobviousness standard and thus the patent should not be enforced. The Court's action is seen by some observers as an indication that it is becoming concerned that the scope of patent enforcement has expanded to the point where it impedes commercial development.

It seems likely that Jefferson would have favored active application of the nonobviousness criterion. He preferred to limit patent awards to the most novel of inventions. He recognized that essentially all inventive work builds upon and extends the efforts of others. The requirement of nonobviousness, even though it is difficult to evaluate, provides an additional safeguard to limit the reach of patents. It is a standard that recognizes and accommodates the evolutionary nature of the process of invention, and for that reason it would likely have appealed to Jefferson.

In modern times, there has been a growing tendency to make the correlation between patentability and value that Jefferson chose not to establish. Today, we often make an assumption that an invention that can be patented has greater value than one that cannot. Although that may certainly be true from the perspective of an inventor who is trying to maximize economic gain from that single invention, the correlation does not necessarily hold when value is assessed from the perspective of the society or even from the perspective of the long-term economic interests of the inventor.

Jefferson perceived a clear distinction between patent rights and value. Although Jefferson saw patents as a method to promote social and economic value, he did not take the position that only patentable work added value to the society. Instead, he believed that patents were appropriate for the most innovative and useful work, but that the work covered by patents continued to require refinement and improvement. Patented works were valuable to society. To realize their full potential value, however, they had to be put into use as quickly and as broadly as possible. That use would generate enhancements and new applications for the products.

Jefferson's focus on utility and novelty had a profound impact on the early patent review process. To assess the utility of an invention, it was necessary to thoroughly understand how the invention was constructed and how it operated. The examiner was required to evaluate models and to demonstrate prototypes. It was a demanding review process, time-consuming and requiring substantial technical facility on the part of the examiner. In addition, the analysis of the novelty of the invention required substantial research, both current and historical. To determine whether the invention was novel, the examiner was forced to review historical records as well as the technical literature of the day. This review, coupled with the testing and demonstration associated with the utility evaluation, made the patent examination process demanding for both the applicant and the examiner.

Although Jefferson was an accomplished scientist and inventor himself, he ultimately found that the demands of the patent application review and examination process were extraordinary. At one level, patent application review required an understanding of a wide range of subjects and technologies. With regard to the patents he and his colleagues were required to consider, Jefferson noted in a 1792 letter to Hugh Williamson that "the subjects are such as would require a great deal of time to understand and do justice by them." Given the range of the demands on his time in his capacity as secretary of state, he acknowledged that he did not have adequate time to consider properly all the requests for patents. Jefferson was seriously troubled that the conflicting demands on his time made him "obliged to give crude and uninformed opinions" on many of the patent applications. He recognized that the patent rights that he and the rest of the Board of Arts controlled were "often valuable, and always deemed so by the authors."

Observers have properly noted that Jefferson did not create U.S. patent law; he did not write the 1790 patent legislation. He did, however, profoundly influence the practice of patent law through his actions while serving on the first Board of Arts. His experience on that first board also gave him practical experience in implementing patent law which he used when offering his opinions during the preparation of the 1793 revisions to the Patent Act. Based on his direct experience reviewing and evaluating the first generation of U.S. patent applications, Jefferson developed strong opinions regarding improvements to the American patent law system.

Largely because he felt that the process of examining patent applications placed a substantial burden on the board, Jefferson advocated a shift to a patent registration process which would register proposed inventions but place less emphasis on their examination. In the 1793 revisions to the Patent Act, Congress responded to some of Jefferson's suggestions by making the process more of a clerical system and less of an oversight and review process. The 1793 act designated the secretary of state as the recipient of all patent applications. Review of those applications was confined to an assessment to determine that the applications met the formalities of filing. There was no longer a review of the substance of the applications. Under the 1793 act, any disputes associated with the substance of patents would be resolved in the federal courts. That shift was altered with the next substantial revision of U.S. patent law, in 1836, when the process was revised to return to a more rigorous substantive review of applications.

One important consequence of a patent process that is more a registration system than an examination and review system is that it tends to shift power from the patent examiner to the courts. A registration system only screens applications based on compliance with the filing formalities of the system. All applications that provide the requisite materials in support of the application will receive a patent. No assessment is made of the merits of the invention prior to award of the patent. Evaluation of the substantive merits of inventions is deferred to the time, if ever, when a patent is enforced. The courts provide the forum in which such disputes will be raised; thus responsibility for examining and assessing the substantive merits of inventions moves to the courts.

There are at least two important concerns that arise with the shift of patent assessment from the Patent Office to the courts. One concern is the competence of judges with respect to the technical evaluations that are at the heart of patent enforcement actions. There is a real basis for concern that many judges who may be called upon to hear these cases have neither the expertise nor the interest to act effectively to resolve these disputes. A second basic concern is that the system places the burden of evaluation of the merits of the patent on the defendants in the patent litigation. The patentees enter those cases in possession of their patents, and the burden then falls on the defendants, the alleged patent infringers, to contest the merits of the patents. Effectively, no screening of the merits of the patent takes place prior to litigation.

The challenges Jefferson and his colleagues encountered while attempting to do justice to the patent applications presented to them continue to be faced by patent examiners today. Examiners would like to invest the effort and other resources necessary to conduct an effective review of proposed inventions including a comprehensive review of the prior art and a rigorous examination of the merits of the inventions. Patent examiners today, as was the case with Jefferson and his colleagues, simply do not have the resources necessary to complete the type of comprehensive examination that the patent process requires. It is worth noting that the scope of today's patent system dwarfs that of Jefferson's time. During his term on the Board of Arts, sixty-seven patents were issued. Today, the U.S. Patent Office processes several hundred thousand patent applications each year. In the years between Jefferson's work on the Board of Arts and today, more than seven million patents have been issued in the United States.

Two common criticisms of the patent approval process today are largely the result of the shortage of resources. One criticism is that the process of reviewing patents is slower than it should be. The second criticism is that patent examiners grant patents for inventions that do not merit patent protection. These concerns were also present in Jefferson's time. To some extent, these problems associated with the patent approval process seem to be inevitable. The consequences of these apparent flaws in the process are profound. Excessively slow processing impedes the development of useful applications for new inventions. Grant of too many weak patents — patents issued for inventions that do not truly merit patent protection — makes it more difficult for the public to access inventions, and it impedes development of new applications for, and refinements of, those patented inventions. Grant of unworthy patents also places increased strain on the courts, the institution that must resolve patent enforcement disputes.

This seemingly inevitable tension between a thorough review of patent applications to prevent issuance of weak patents on the one hand and a more ministerial process that permits greater efficiency while using fewer resources on the other is a major reason why the patent process seems to shift back and forth between times of greater and lesser rigor. When thorough reviews are conducted, the process requires greater resources and is more cumbersome, thus leading to the criticism of inefficiency. In response, changes are made to make the process less rigorous and more efficient. The result of those changes is commonly issuance of weaker patents, which in turn causes inefficiency in the patent administration process. Through the years, we continue to see the patent process move back and forth between these two poles, and that movement seems likely to continue into the foreseeable future.

PATENT ENFORCEMENT

Obtaining a patent is only the first step in the process of exercising proprietary rights. After a patent has been issued by the government, the task of maintaining and enforcing it falls to the recipient of the patent, the patentee. The administrative process of maintaining a patent can be cumbersome. The litigation necessary to enforce patent rights can be expensive. The patent enables the patentee to stop others from manufacturing or using the invention; but it is the responsibility of the patentee to identify and to take action against any patent infringer, and the patentee bears the cost associated with such enforcement.

The patent process that was developing in England during Jefferson's time was cumbersome and costly. As a result, use of patents was generally practical only for businesses and inventors with well-funded patrons. At least in part in reaction to the English system, the Americans attempted to make their patent system more accessible for individual inventors. The American patent process was significantly less expensive and easier to navigate for an inventor than was the process in England.

The impact of the patent enforcement process on the overall effectiveness of the system remains an important issue today. The practical need to obtain, maintain, and enforce patent rights in several different countries makes the cost of patenting extremely high. This growing burden associated with patent administration means that a patent-based commercial strategy has become less feasible for individuals and small businesses than it was in the past. Increasingly, only larger businesses have access to the financial resources necessary to maintain patents and to sustain the litigation necessary to enforce them. It is now common for larger companies to invest in substantial patent portfolios to help protect themselves from litigation risk. The companies negotiate cross-license arrangements with other companies when there are patent disputes. This enables the companies to avoid costly litigation and permits them to continue to use the technologies of others without being required to make monetary payments.

Patenting becomes a form of competitive insurance for larger companies. In this environment, however, individuals and small companies do not have the resources necessary to compete, and they are thus placed at a notable competitive disadvantage. When the patent system becomes more burdensome and expensive, it places those inventors that have access to greater technical expertise and financial resources at a competitive advantage.

Proliferation of weak patents adds significantly to the operational burdens of the federal courts. The number of patent infringement cases has increased substantially as the number of patents has grown and as patentees place greater commercial emphasis on their patents. Patent litigation becomes more complex and more protracted as the number of weak patents increases, and the enforcement actions become forums in which the validity and enforceability of the patents are challenged by the defendants as a matter of course.

As the judicial process became more important to patent enforcement, court procedures began to have major substantive impact on the effectiveness of patent rights. A modern example is the use of preliminary injunctions in advance of court action on the merits of a case. Patent and other intellectual property enforcement cases now commonly arise when there is some ongoing commercial activity that is alleged to involve infringement of an intellectual property right. When a patentee goes to court alleging that the manufacturer of a product is infringing on a patent, the patentee now commonly asks the court to order the defendant to cease manufacture and sale of the product, pending resolution of the case on its merits.

Courts have the ability to issue a preliminary injunction temporarily stopping the sale of the allegedly infringing products if they determine that it is likely that the patentee will prevail in the case on the merits. Courts now routinely issue such injunctions. In part, the decision to issue a preliminary injunction requires the court to make an advance estimate of the relative merits of the parties in the case. The choice regarding an injunction is a procedural decision for a court, but it is a decision that can have major commercial implications. In some instances, the injunction can cause commercial damage to the defendant that is severe enough to make it impossible for the defendant to mount a defense in the case, or to cause the defendant to cease business operations.

Preliminary injunctions provide a mechanism that enables intellectual property owners to enforce their rights through the courts, even before the courts have fully evaluated the merits of their case. Thus, if there is a well-financed patentee and a financially weaker defendant, it is possible that the patentee may be able to drive the defendant out of business even before a court reaches a final decision on the merits of the infringement claim. By relying on the courts as the key venue for evaluation of the merits of patents and other forms of intellectual property, enforcement of intellectual property rights is substantially affected by the ability and interest of the courts, and by the ability of both the holder of the intellectual property rights and the defendant to finance litigation. In effect, the costs associated with operation of the intellectual property rights system are substantially shifted from the government to the private parties who own and use the intellectual property.

THE ROLE OF PATENTS

The concept of patents, which was based on a history of patents as monopoly rights awarded in an effort to facilitate infusion of new products for the overall benefit of society, was evolving during Jefferson's time. For one thing, that evolution involved growing public concern about overly broad monopoly rights. During the eighteenth and nineteenth centuries, public sentiment turned increasingly wary of broad government grants of monopoly rights. Jefferson shared the growing public concern with regard to monopolies, noting in a 1788 letter to James Madison that "monopolies are sacrifices of the many to the few." Yet he also recognized, in a 1790 letter to Benjamin Vaughan, that patents had "given a spring of invention beyond my conception." While he acknowledged that many of the patents were "trifling," he noted that "there are some of great consequence." Thus although Jefferson was concerned about the use of monopolies to encourage invention, he recognized that patents did provide incentives for inventive work.

The role of patents was also evolving as the public began to recognize that patents provided a mechanism to transform innovation into commercial gain. Increasingly, patents were seen as the link between science and commerce. A growing number of technical professionals, including James Watt and Oliver Evans, recognized that patents had potentially significant economic value. To the extent that patents could be obtained and broadly enforced, they offered the potential for noteworthy profits. Inventors began to see the process of patenting as part of the process of commercialization.

The scope of patents was also evolving. Traditionally, patents were associated with specific products, commonly ones that had not previously been available in the market. Increasingly, patents became associated with technologies and processes, not simply existing products. To the extent that those technologies and processes could be adapted to a range of products and applications, the scope of influence and control provided by patents was notably expanded. That expanded scope offered the opportunity for greater earnings from the patent, but also made it more difficult to coordinate the rights of patent holders, new inventors, and consumers.

This evolution in the role of patents affected the established public policy balance. Although there had long been public concern about monopolies, they had been justified as serving the public interest, since awarding those monopoly rights provided the necessary incentive and opportunity for useful new products to enter the marketplace. Except for such monopoly rights, useful new products available elsewhere might be delayed in entering the market. If the scope of the monopoly rights granted as patents expanded significantly, however, the power of the owner of the patent would also grow.

An important issue beginning to be recognized during Jefferson's time was the challenge of providing enough incentive and opportunity to facilitate prompt introduction of new technologies and products to the society without placing too much power in the hands of the patent owner. If granted too much power, the patent owner would effectively control public access to the new technologies and products and could wield that power in ways that advanced the patent owner's private interests without serving the broader public interest. The origin of patent rights was based on an exchange between the government and the developer of a new and useful product. The patent was the mechanism through which the benefits of the new product could be realized by the public most quickly. Patents were not originally viewed as a reward for the product developer but were, instead, a means of obtaining access to the products for the public.

The scope of patent rights is influenced both by the range of inventions for which patents are awarded and by the extent to which the patents, once issued, are enforced. Jefferson and his colleagues on that first Board of Arts adopted a review and examination process that attempted to put rigorous demands on inventors who were seeking patents. They sought to award patents only for the most useful and unique inventions. This approach was entirely consistent with the view that monopolies should be authorized only when they offer the clear prospect of bringing new benefits for the public.

The 1793 version of the Patent Act altered the patent environment by changing the process of reviewing patent applications. By making that process more of a registration process than a substantive review, the act caused the monopolies represented by patents to become far more widespread. The only instances when there would be a substantive review of a patent would be in cases where there was a dispute. That dispute would be handled by the courts. The 1793 Patent Act effectively eliminated substantive examination of inventions during the patent application review process. Although Jefferson was not the sole cause of this fundamental change in American patent law, he was an active supporter. His support for the change was based upon his direct experience as an overworked patent examiner.

Jefferson was willing to accept the limited grant of patent rights, yet he did not believe those rights had any basis in natural law principles. In his 1813 letter to Isaac McPherson discussing the Oliver Evans milling technology patents, Jefferson noted that there was widespread support for the notion that no individual has a natural law right to ownership of land. With that principle as a base, Jefferson went on to contend that no inventor has a natural right claim of ownership of his invention. Societies may choose to grant an ownership interest, but that interest does not, in Jefferson's view, arise from any natural law foundation.

Also worth noting is the increasing interaction between patent law and other legal disciplines. Today, for instance, patent law commonly and extensively interacts with legal disciplines including antitrust law and international trade law. This mingling of patent law with other fields of law is not unique to our time: patent law in colonial America was connected to issues of international trade, just as it is today. Admittedly, the interaction between patent law and other legal disciplines is far more extensive today than it was in Jefferson's time, but it is important to note that there is a long history of recognizing that patent law structure and enforcement have a noteworthy impact on a wide range of important national legal and public policy issues. It is well recognized today, and has been from colonial times, that the application of patent law, and other forms of intellectual property law, has significant consequences for other important national policy objectives including economic competition and international commerce. It is important to recognize and to accommodate those connections between intellectual property law and other legal and public policy objectives.

Jefferson's pioneering work on the Board of Arts extended his practical experience with intellectual property rights. In that capacity, he played an important role in the development of American patent law practice and procedure. In addition, he gained direct experience in addressing the fundamental challenges faced by all patent authorities. Jefferson confronted the basic challenge of fairly and effectively administering the patent process. He understood the very practical difficulties associated with continuing efforts to balance incentives for inventors with preservation of access to the works created by those inventors.

FIVE

JEFFERSON BATTLES
THE PATENT TROLLS

atent law professionals often apply a vivid term to those who obtain patents, then simply wait for others to infringe upon them. Called patent "trolls," instead of actively moving to make use of their inventions by developing them themselves or by licensing others to develop them, they let their patents sit unused. As time passes, they monitor commerce with an eye toward parties who may be using the patented inventions in various products. When they find such use, the trolls contact the users and demand payment of license fees as compensation for permission to make use of the protected inventions. If the contacted parties refuse to pay, the trolls may choose to go to court to enforce their patents.

An important factor behind the patent troll strategy is the assumption that parties who have already incorporated the patented technology into successful commercial products will take whatever action is necessary to ensure that they can continue to market their product. The trolls prefer situations where the path of least resistance for the users of the patented technology is to share some of the revenues from the sale of the product with the owner of the patent. Litigation is not the desired outcome for the trolls. Instead, they would prefer that the users of the technology make a business judgment that it is more economically efficient to share a portion of the profits with the patent owner.

No one in Jefferson's time was acting as a patent troll, under our modern definition of that term. There were, however, a growing number of inventors who were beginning to integrate licensing of rights to use patents into a deliberate commercial strategy. Instead of relying solely on their ability to manufacture and sell their inventions, these inventors chose to add an additional revenue stream to their businesses. They continued to manufacture and sell their inventions, yet they also allowed others to make use of their patented inventions in exchange for payment of a fee, which we now call a license fee or royalty. One example of this new breed of inventor was Oliver Evans, and his path crossed with that of Thomas Jefferson with over a patent associated with the operation of mills.

The interaction between Evans and Jefferson provided Jefferson with another set of practical experiences involving the management of intellectual property rights. To Evans, Jefferson and others were patent infringers. To Jefferson, the patent commercialization strategy adopted by Evans constituted overreaching and misuse of patent rights. The experience gave Jefferson direct understanding of the impact of commercial patenting strategies and added another level of depth to Jefferson's practical knowledge of intellectual property rights management issues. The Evans case also illustrates the extent to which Jefferson failed to recognize that commercialization of the process of invention was rapidly developing into a dominant model for research and development.

JEFFERSON VERSUS OLIVER EVANS

Oliver Evans was a highly successful and well-known early American inventor. He is perhaps best known as one of the American pioneers in the development of steam engine technology. In 1790 Evans received a U.S. patent for an automated milling process. The Evans patent, the third patent issued by Jefferson's Board of Arts, covered the use of bucket elevators, conveyor belts, and Archimedean screws to create a mill that could operate on an automated basis. Louis Hunter has characterized the Evans mill technology as "a milestone in the history of mechanization." After receiving his patent, Evans approached a number of mill owners and accused them of using milling technology covered by his patent. Evans requested payment of royalties for the right to use the patented technology in their mills. The millers refused to pay, and Evans decided to litigate to enforce his patent.

In federal court in Pennsylvania, Evans sued claiming infringement of his patent by a group of millers. The court concluded that the Evans patent was invalid. Reviewing the record, the court determined that the description of the Evans invention provided in the patent was inadequate. Since the amount in question in the case was less than the threshold value required to permit an appeal of the decision, the patent was held to be unenforceable, and Evans did not have the right to appeal that finding.

Evans petitioned Congress seeking relief from the court's decision. He argued that, to the extent that the description of the invention included in the patent was inadequate, the fault was not his but instead resided with the government. Evans claimed that he had submitted a more complete description of the invention as part of his application, but that additional material was not included in the patent. Millers, the users of the Evans technology, opposed congressional action to grant Evans relief. Despite his persistent efforts, it was January 1808 before Evans was able to obtain congressional action. At that time, Congress enacted legislation that authorized the secretary of state to issue a patent to Evans.

There was some uncertainty as to the impact of the Evans legislation on users of the milling technology. The act provided that no one who had licensed the technology from Evans under the original patent grant would be required to renew or extend the license. Presumably, this provision was intended to account for the fact that the term of the original patent had already expired by the time the new patent was granted. The act also provided that no one who had been using the Evans technology prior to the grant of the new patent would be liable for damages for that prior use.

The question that arose after the new patent was authorized by Congress was the financial obligations of those prior users if they continued to use the technology after the grant of the new patent to Evans. The U.S. Supreme Court addressed that issue in the 1815 case *Evans v. Jordan.* The Court concluded that all who had placed the technology in operation prior to the grant of the new patent would be obligated to pay a license to continue to use the technology after the grant of the new patent. Failure to pay such a license fee would subject the continuing user to monetary damages for infringement.

Jefferson was among the group of millers who had placed the Evans technology into operation before the grant of the new patent. He objected to the Oliver Evans patents in part because he believed that they covered inventions that had existed long before Evans worked on them. Jefferson presented his case against the Evans patents in an 1813 letter to Isaac McPherson. According to Jefferson, the elevator and conveyor patents obtained by Evans included technology that had been known and used for centuries before Evans was even born. Jefferson noted that the ancient civilizations of Egypt and Persia had used strings of buckets to move water and other material. Jefferson considered the devices and process included in the Evans patents to be well-established prior art, and on that basis he did not believe that Evans should have been able to obtain the patents he was trying to enforce.

Jefferson was also critical of the Evans patents because he considered them to be too broad in scope. He did not agree with the notion that a single patent holder should be in a position to limit a wide range of applications for a technology based on a patent granted for one particular application. Writing to McPherson in 1813, Jefferson argued that the owner of a device should have the right to make use of that device "for any use of which it is susceptible, and that this ought not be taken from him and given to a monopolist." Similarly, he objected to the use of a patent to restrict development of modified versions of the device in question that made use of different materials or different designs.

Jefferson objected to use of a single patent to cover a wide range of variations in design and application. He did not, however, specifically address the situation that his approach would likely have generated. The narrow patent scope advocated by Jefferson would likely have invited multiple patent applications, each covering a different variation on the original invention. Thus if, as Jefferson suggested in his letter to McPherson, a patent for manufacturing a plowshare out of cast iron should not cover the manufacture of a plowshare out of wrought iron, one would expect that inventors would present separate patent applications for the cast iron and wrought iron versions.

Jefferson did not want to encourage multiple patents, each covering a slight variation of an original invention. He did not want to create an environment in which there could be a patent for a cast iron plowshare and another for a wood version. Yet he was also uncomfortable granting a single broad patent that would permit a single patentee to control a wide range of different versions of the original product. Jefferson did not address the question of what will happen if one of those patents is granted. If the first inventor receives a patent for the cast iron version of the plowshare, and no additional patents are granted for versions made of different materials or slightly different designs, the owner of the cast iron patent would presumably seek to enforce the patent against those who make use of the variations of the original invention. This is essentially the position taken by Oliver Evans with respect to the milling technologies. Presumably, Jefferson would respond, as he did in the case of Evans, that no patents should be issued.

Jefferson's objections to the Evans patent are difficult to reconcile with the fact that his Board of Arts granted the patent in the first place. As much as he might argue, in 1813, that the Evans work was not novel, he and his colleagues had reviewed the Evans work in 1790 and considered it worthy of a patent at that time. This substantially different perspective on the Evans work over time may, at least in part, be attributed to Jefferson's reconsidering the impact of aggressive assertion of patent rights. In 1790 active enforcement of patent rights for commercial purposes was in its early stages of development. By 1813 it was a strategy that was widely applied.

Moreover, Jefferson did not seem to acknowledge that part of the reason that Evans resorted to congressional relief for his patent rights was an apparent administrative oversight that took place during Jefferson's time on the Board of Arts. Evans was unable to enforce his patent because it did not include an adequate description of his invention. It appears that the failure to include an adequate invention description was the fault of the Patent Office, not the inventor, since Evans claimed he provided the material with his application, and there was apparently enough of a description to satisfy the board that the application formalities had been met.

The court interpretation that invalidated the Evans patent could also have placed at risk other patents issued by Jefferson's Board of Arts. It is unclear whether the apparent failure to incorporate an adequate description of the invention into the Evans patent was only a problem for that particular patent or a more widespread problem. The small number of patents issued by the Board of Arts at that time and the fact that Evans seems to have been one of the few inventors who actively sought to enforce his patents limited the impact of the documentation problem identified in the Evans case.

Jefferson's dispute with Oliver Evans illustrates two important aspects of his approach to intellectual property rights. The dispute underscores Jefferson's belief that patent rights should be as limited in scope and application as possible. It also highlights Jefferson's concern that patent rights should not thwart the development of new applications and enhancements for existing devices and processes. Although an active inventor in his own right, Jefferson never pursued patents for any of his work. This approach was entirely consistent with his belief that advances should be widely disseminated for public use as rapidly as possible. Jefferson's preference for this open approach to inventions made him wary of those who opted for a more assertive proprietary model with regard to their work.

Note that Evans was forced to work very hard to derive commercial gain from his mill patent. The court's refusal to enforce his patent made it difficult for him to obtain any licensing revenue during the original term of his patent. Only after years of fighting for congressional action was he able to clear his patent rights and require license payments. He thought that his milling technology would make him wealthy, and although he did eventually achieve prosperity fueled by licensing earnings from the mill technology and a variety of other successful patents, it took him many years of hard work. This history is not quite the classic model of the modern patent troll. Jefferson seemed to ignore completely this aspect of commercial invention. He did not recognize or appreciate the extent to which the process of commercial invention is a difficult one to execute effectively. Jefferson displayed no sympathy for those who attempt to support themselves economically based on their inventive work.

Jefferson's greatest concern when an inventor such as Oliver Evans actively enforced his patent rights was that the inventor would prevent the invention from being placed into practical use. This, to Jefferson, was the worst possible outcome. He was not opposed to inventors deriving income from their inventions, he was opposed to them using patent rights to keep their work out of productive use. No rights of inventors should ever justify that denial of public access. One might reasonably suggest that Jefferson would have found many advantages to the use of compulsory licenses for certain forms of intellectual property. Compulsory licenses require that patentees make their inventions available for use by others, subject to reasonable licensing fees. The compulsory license approach ensures that users have access to patented works, yet it also ensures that the owners of those patents receive reasonable compensation for the use of their work. Such a balance would likely have pleased Jefferson.

THE SCOPE OF PATENT ENFORCEMENT

Jefferson's experience as the target of a patent enforcement initiative made him even more vigorous in his belief that patents should be enforced as narrowly as possible. As an alleged patent infringer, Jefferson encountered directly the consequences of the rights that he had granted as a member of the Board of Arts. He saw firsthand how aggressive enforcement of broad patents can impede integration of innovations into daily personal and commercial activities.

That direct experience provided substantial insight into the frustration felt by those who would work to refine, diversify, and advance existing works. Jefferson felt the sting of patent law's ability to deny access to essential materials. His motivation for using the proprietary materials was need, not economic gain. The Evans technology provided the most effective mill equipment, which Jefferson, and many other farmers, required. This experience, coupled with his thorough knowledge of patent law and his appreciation of the power of invention, gave Jefferson a full understanding of all aspects of the patent law.

The Evans dispute may also have caused Jefferson to appreciate more fully the increasingly commercial nature of patents and invention. His encounter with Evans, an inventor actively engaged in commercial development of patented technology, may have encouraged him to reconsider his prior support for a patent system based on registration. To the extent that such a system shifts patent examination duties to the courts, it can result in more patent litigation and an increasing burden on both patentees and users of the patented technologies.

Part of Jefferson's frustration with respect to the Evans patents was that he was generally sympathetic to inventors. Jefferson knew, from direct experience, the joy of invention. He had the passion to apply knowledge creatively in pursuit of useful solutions to everyday challenges. He was not, however, eager to exploit his inventive work commercially. Jefferson the inventor never sought patent protection, but instead made every effort to have his innovations disseminated for use as widely as possible, as quickly as possible. Encountering a fellow inventor, and a highly skilled one at that, who seemed to place a greater priority on commercial gain from inventions than on rapid dissemination of those inventions into practice, Jefferson was irritated.

Despite Jefferson's ire, the commercialization strategy applied by Evans was becoming increasingly common during Jefferson's lifetime. The strategy of actively asserting proprietary rights over inventions and converting those rights into a source of revenue was gaining recognition as an effective commercial plan. The ability to obtain patent rights and to enforce those rights was the heart of such a business strategy. Inventors no longer relied solely on their own ability to manufacture and distribute products based on their inventions. Instead, they could also look to compensation from others who wanted to make use of the patented technology.

It is interesting to consider Jefferson's encounter with Oliver Evans in the context of his evaluation of the efforts of Jacob Isaacks to commercialize his desalination technology. When examining the Isaacks technology, Jefferson and his colleagues made a thorough review of the prior art in that field. They concluded that although the work of Isaacks seemed effective and had potential utility, it was not novel, and there was a strong likelihood that other technologies could also be effective. Jefferson recognized that it would be appropriate for Isaacks to attempt to commercialize his technology, but he believed that the marketplace should determine the success of that technology, not a government-provided grant of exclusivity.

The ability of Oliver Evans to obtain a position of exclusivity through his patent rights put Evans in precisely the competitive position that Jefferson sought to prevent for Isaacks. In Jefferson's view, the Evans technology was not novel, and his broad assertion of patent rights was inappropriate. Nonetheless, Evans was able to assert his proprietary claims by virtue of his patent rights. This result was contrary to Jefferson's perception of how invention and innovation ought to progress. As noted above, Jefferson would have no quarrel with Evans, or any other inventor, developing and commercializing technologies. His objection arises when the inventor is able to prevent productive use of a technology by obtaining patent rights for work that is not truly novel.

The conflicting positions taken by Evans and Jefferson with respect to the mill patent are made all the more complicated by the fact that Jefferson and his colleagues were the people who granted Evans his patent. In effect, Jefferson gave Evans the rights that he sought to enforce against Jefferson and others. Although Jefferson makes it clear that he does not believe that the Evans patent should be enforceable, he does not explain why he permitted the patent to be issued in the first place.

One possible explanation is that Jefferson had not anticipated the development of a commercialization strategy that relied so heavily on patent enforcement. When he was involved in patent review during his service on the Board of Arts, use of active commercialization strategies for patents was only in its early stages, and litigation to enforce patents was not particularly common. Perhaps when Jefferson and his colleagues were considering those first patent applications, they did not expect to see the patents aggressively enforced in the manner of Evans and a growing number of his fellow inventors. Part of Jefferson's criticism of Evans is perhaps a reflection of his growing concern that the new patent commercialization strategy could dramatically impede the process of continuing innovation.

Jefferson had no real appreciation for the mechanics of the process of commercialization of inventions. He was thoroughly familiar with the process of technical refinement necessary to transform an invention into a useful device, but he was blind to the economic and commercial incentives and transactions necessary to support the technical refinements. This is perhaps not surprising for a man who had such great difficulty managing his personal financial resources and transactions. Jefferson was far more comfortable with the notion of the gentleman or scholarly inventor than he was with the commercial or industrial inventor. He had more in common with the part-time, amateur inventor than he did with inventors like Evans who conducted their research and development work as part of a deliberate commercial strategy.

Jefferson seemed to believe that continuous sharing of information regarding inventions and new technologies would be sufficient to move those innovations into commercial use. He saw the commercialization challenge as largely a matter of information and knowledge sharing. He did not appreciate that the commercialization process required more extensive economic incentives. Jefferson had the luxury of adopting this position, since he did not rely on his inventions for income or competitive advantage.

During the 1800s, however, a rapidly growing number of individuals and enterprises began to rely on their inventive work as commercial assets. Inventors including Oliver Evans, Eli Whitney, and James Watt pioneered a commercial strategy that relied upon intellectual property as a source of revenue and competitive strength. These pioneer commercial inventors soon discovered that the process of transforming a new technology into a useful and popular product was a long and expensive one.

Jefferson had no understanding of, or appreciation for, the challenges facing commercial inventors. This fundamental disconnect created a clear rift between Jefferson and the proponents of the modern strategy of intellectual property commercialization. For Jefferson, the commercial inventors were driven by greed to assert overly broad proprietary rights encompassing work that was not original. From the perspective of the commercial inventors, aggressive assertion of intellectual property rights was the only mechanism available through which they could derive economic returns sufficient to enable them to sustain their business model based on continuing invention and technological advances. The rift between Jefferson and the commercial inventors that opened in the nineteenth century continues to pose important public policy and commercial challenges today.

The twentieth century saw the strategy of commercial invention rise to dominance. The process that started with individual commercial inventors eventually lead to major research organizations inspired by prominent inventors such as Morse, Edison, and Bell, and later to the establishment of corporate research groups, including those at AT&T, IBM, and GE.

The process of invention plays a profound and vital role in the economic development of the United States and countries around the world. Largely because of this economic impact, the strategy of commercial invention and intellectual property commercialization has significantly influenced the patent system in the United States and abroad. That system now offers substantially greater incentives for commercial inventors than it did during Jefferson's time, but in spite of the rise in prominence of commercial invention, many of the goals expressed by Jefferson for intellectual property rights remain important and relevant today. The dominance of commercialization has not negated the concerns expressed by Jefferson.

SIX

JEFFERSON AND THE CHALLENGES OF INVENTION AND INNOVATION

M
any of the goals and concerns expressed by Jefferson with respect to knowledge, invention, and innovation remain relevant today. Although it would not be fair to assert which positions Jefferson would support on the specific policy issues of today regarding invention and innovation, it is both reasonable and instructive to examine how Jefferson's approach to those issues is reflected in today's debates. It is also reasonable to turn to Jefferson's experiences and actions as a useful model for the opportunities and challenges available to political leaders to influence in constructive ways efforts to facilitate creativity, invention, and innovation.

Jefferson's experience illustrates the importance of recognizing and retaining the broader economic, social, and political context within which intellectual property rights are established and managed. His appreciation that intellectual property rights have an impact far beyond their effects on individual developers and users of intellectual property is a valuable lesson for us today.

INVENTION AND ECONOMIC DEVELOPMENT

Jefferson recognized that there was a connection between invention and economic development. He noted that a young country like the United States was dependent on the scientific work conducted by other, more established, countries. In 1821 Jefferson wrote that "in an infant country like ours, we must depend for improvement on science of other countries, longer established, possessing better means, and more advanced than we are." He added that "to prohibit us from the benefit of that foreign light is to consign us to darkness." We see a similar dynamic at work today. Developing countries are largely dependent on scientific and technological advances pioneered in more mature nations, just as the United States was in the eighteenth and nineteenth centuries.

America, in Jefferson's time, was a developing country. He recognized that all developing countries must rely on their more advanced neighbors as sources of science and technical advances, until they are able to establish the foundation of knowledge and expertise necessary to become active contributing members to the global inventory of information and innovation. Yet he also recognized that the young America had already developed fields of special technical expertise and that the nation was rapidly developing a much broader range of technical knowledge across its population than had the Europeans. In a 1785 letter to Charles Bellini, Jefferson noted that in knowledge of science the majority of the European population was "two centuries behind ours"; however, among the educated elites the Europeans were "half a dozen years before us."

He had high hopes for American world leadership in certain fields of science. In an 1807 letter to Caspar Wistar, Jefferson expressed his aspiration that American medical science would one day lead the world. He believed that Europeans made use of American innovations, both legitimately and illegitimately. For instance, in a 1787 letter to St. John de Crèvecoeur, Jefferson referred to the recent grant of an English patent for a process of creating a wheel out of a single piece of wood. The patent was of interest to Jefferson as an example of a piece of American technology expropriated by the English.

It should not surprise us that Jefferson, although recognizing the clear advantage that more established countries held over the United States with respect to science and technology, expressed confidence in both the current and future technical capabilities of this country. His belief in the importance of dissemination and sharing of knowledge suggested to him that open societies are more likely to obtain, absorb, and apply useful information more quickly than their closed counterpart nations. If America continued to promote and protect the free flow of information, it would rapidly grow to rival more established nations in fields where knowledge developed quickly. If America effectively connected with the world networks of knowledge flow, it would rapidly benefit from their content and would soon generate and contribute its own content to advance those networks.

It is easy to see why Jefferson was opposed to actions in the United States and abroad that could disrupt the flow of information within and between countries. The flow of people and ideas between Europe and America was an essential part of America's future development. Any interruption of that flow would, in Jefferson's view, have an adverse impact on the United States. For example, one of the concerns expressed by Jefferson concerning the Alien and Sedition Acts was their potential use to keep independent thinkers, including scientists, out of the United States. Jefferson was particularly concerned that the law would be used against the scientist Joseph Priestley. Priestley was one of the world's leading chemists, but he was also a political and social activist. Jefferson feared that Priestley was exactly the type of freethinking individual who would be harmed by the acts.

Today we continue to face concerns regarding legal initiatives that may restrict the flow of scientists and technology professionals between the United States and the rest of the world. For example, current immigration laws that make it more difficult for scientists, technology experts, and students to enter the United States, to work in this country, and to remain here for significant periods of time can restrict the essential free flow of information that advances scientific research and technological innovation. Such restriction has adverse economic, political, and social implications for the United States.

Jefferson and his colleagues understood the importance of the movement of scientists and engineers between nations. They recognized that the movement of people was often more important than the movement of technology or information. When a specific technology or some particular example of know-how moves to another country, there is value associated with that transfer for the nation that receives it. Yet when a highly able person moves to another nation, that nation receives not only all that individual has accomplished in the past but also everything he or she will accomplish in the future.

In addition to the issue of the transnational flow of scientists and engineers, there is also the issue of the movement of technical professionals from business to business. Such movement took place in Jefferson's time, although on a far smaller scale than that of today. At present, many businesses attempt to use legal mechanisms to restrict that movement. For example, contracts such as noncompetition agreements and nondisclosure agreements are widely used in industries where departing employees could take vital business information with them. Companies who lose their employees to competitors are rightfully concerned that those employees will take proprietary information that will be used against the former employer. The departing employees argue that it is unreasonable to prevent them from providing their services to other employers. Given his respect for the importance of the free exchanges of ideas and people, it seems likely that Jefferson would have been concerned about widespread use of such noncompetition and nondisclosure agreements.

Throughout this book we have addressed the challenge of effectively balancing proprietary rights with rights of access and use. Intellectual property law is a never-ending effort to balance those often conflicting objectives. It seems quite clear that Jefferson consistently favored erring on the side of more open access to intellectual property. Part of his reasoning was that more open access enables more people to be involved in the process of evaluating, refining, and expanding the overall base of knowledge. That broader participation helps to increase the pace of development. This philosophy was reasonable and productive in Jefferson's time, and it remains so today.

THE POWER OF TECHNICAL STANDARDS

An interesting and significant aspect of Jefferson's philosophy was his appreciation for the importance and value of standards. He was highly active in discussions on the development of standards for weights and measures as well as for currency. He was also involved in efforts to establish a rational system for land surveying as part of the first national effort in the United States to distribute the lands of the Western Territory. Additionally, he was involved in early efforts to make the process of allocating congressional representation more fair and reasonable. In each instance, Jefferson attempted to create systems of technical standards and processes that were fair, effective, and rational.

Jefferson appreciated the potential impact of standards on both commercial and personal activities. The challenge of developing and enforcing appropriate standards remains critically important today and may well prove to be still more important in the future. Jefferson was one of the first Americans to focus on the importance of standards across a wide range of activities. It is possible that at least part of his concern for the development of standards rose from his interest in numbers and his faith in the utility of mathematics as a means of analysis and problem resolution. His appreciation for the power of standards may also have been influenced by his faith in the effectiveness of the scientific method of inquiry. His scientific and technical work helped him to understand the vital importance of uniformity and consistency in experimentation, data collection, and analysis. The pursuit of uniformity and consistency requires effective standardization.

His recognition of the long-term significance of technical standards seems quite modern. He understood that technical standards must be accepted by the public, and to be accepted they must be trusted. That trust can only develop if the standards are established though an open and rational process. The public must understand the process through which the standards are developed, and it must accept that process as a rational and fair one. In addition, the standards must be enforceable, and they must be applied fairly and consistently. Jefferson's appreciation of the significance of technical standards and the need to focus on their integrity provides important lessons for our time as well.

In 1790 Congress requested that Jefferson examine the issue of the establishment of a uniform system for weights, measures, and currency. At that time, the United States did not have a consistent system to ensure that weights and measurements were uniform across the states. Absent such a uniform system, interstate commercial transactions were difficult to manage, which had a negative impact on commerce in the country. Congress wanted Jefferson to recommend a plan to establish a reasonable and effective set of standards for the entire nation. The charge presented from Congress to Jefferson was to "prepare and report a proper plan or plans for establishing uniformity in the currency, weights, and measures of the United States."

As Gary Wills has noted, Jefferson did not want to build American standards of measurement on the systems already in place in Europe. Instead, he wanted to make use of the most current knowledge to create the most accurate possible measurement system. The starting point for such a system was the unit for measuring length. A disciple of Newton, Jefferson was convinced that his principles of motion would provide the most effective foundation for the standards of measurement. As Newton had discovered, motion offered the potential for accuracy, precision, and uniformity that no other system could provide.

Jefferson wanted to base the measurement system on Newton's discovery that a pendulum placed at a specific latitude on the globe would have an oscillation unique to that latitude. The different level of force of gravity exerted at each different latitude could be used to establish a unit of length that could be replicated over and over again. The standard of length would be set as the distance of the oscillation of a pendulum of a given length at a specified latitude. The appeal of this approach, to Jefferson, was that the length standard could be consistently measured, and it would have as its source natural motion identified through an understanding of basic principles of nature instead of an arbitrarily selected object.

Jefferson's approach was more difficult to implement than he had anticipated. One major challenge was that the motion described by a string-and-bob pendulum was an arc instead of a straight line. Precise measurement of the distance prescribed by the pendulum would thus require measurement of the arc, instead of a line. Another problem was the need to identify a uniform shape and weight for the bobs used with the pendulum. Uniformity of the bobs was necessary to achieve consistent motion, but any choice of bob weight and shape was an arbitrary selection, and this type of arbitrary component was precisely what Jefferson sought to avoid. There was also the observation that the force of gravity was not necessarily precisely uniform at all points even along the same latitude. In addition, temperature variations would affect the length of the pendulum and must thus be accounted for in the description of the standard.

Jefferson attempted to describe his proposal in a report to Congress. The report that Jefferson submitted to Congress later in 1790 has been characterized by Andro Linklater as "a formidable feat of intellectual application." The report discusses the principles of physics and mathematics that favor use of the pendulum to establish a standard of length. As I. B. Cohen has noted, however, Jefferson's emphasis on the technical justification for such a system rendered the report largely inaccessible to the general reader.

Jefferson had intended that the standard of length, developed through the pendulum process, would then be used as the basis for standards for capacity and weight. He proposed a standard of capacity equal to one cubic foot. He called this base standard a bushel. He recommended a system of weight based on an ounce, set as the weight of a cube of rainwater constituting one-tenth of a cubic foot.

Jefferson's proposals were not adopted. Although intellectually elegant, they proved to be too complex for Congress and the public to embrace, and there were noteworthy concerns as to the operational feasibility of the standards. Nevertheless, Jefferson's efforts to devise an accurate and rational set of standards for measurement provide important insight into his appreciation for the importance of uniform technical specifications.

The process Jefferson used to develop his proposal for measurement standards is also instructive. Jefferson relied heavily on his knowledge network, especially his old friend and colleague David Rittenhouse. Rittenhouse served as a sounding board for Jefferson as he tried to structure a measurement standard based on pendulum oscillation. Rittenhouse's deep understanding of Newtonian principles, along with his practical skills as a craftsman of scientific instruments and equipment, made him an exceptionally helpful adviser for Jefferson on this project.

Jefferson also addressed issues of uniform standards in the effort to establish a national currency. During the early days of the nation, different states applied different values to their currency. As one would expect, this lack of consistency and uniformity hampered the efficiency of commercial transactions that spanned state borders. At the time, the official unit of currency was the British pound. In practice, however, the pound had a different value in the different states. In addition, French, Spanish, Portuguese, and other national currencies were in wide use in early America. This mixture of currencies made the challenge of valuation yet more complex.

In an effort to address the lack of uniformity in American currency, Robert Morris proposed establishment of a uniform American currency valued at a fraction of one penny. In 1784 Jefferson opposed the Morris plan. He argued that the Morris standard was set at a value that was too small to be efficient. Instead, he recommended that the standard unit of currency, the dollar, be set to a standard of eleven-twelfths of an ounce of pure silver. The silver content, combined with one-twelfth of an ounce of alloy, would establish the dollar coin at a weight of one ounce.

Jefferson also proposed that the dollar be subdivided into units of value based on the decimal system. American dollars would thus be divided into subunits of tenths, hundredths, and thousandths. Recognizing the significance that a standard of currency held both for commercial life and for social order, he wanted to establish a system of currency that would be both efficient and convenient. Congress adopted Jefferson's proposal in 1785.

In the case of the currency, Jefferson applied an approach that was somewhat different from what he had used for the standards of measurement. For currency, Jefferson focused on both rationality and operational convenience. The currency system he supported had a rational basis, but it was also easy for the public to understand and convenient to place into operation. His proposals for measurement standards were theoretically sound but quite difficult to explain and to implement. His success at having his currency proposal adopted, in contrast to his inability to bring the measurement standard into operation, rested largely on its firmer connection to practical use.

Jefferson's interest in standards is also evident in the debate over standards of land measurement. In 1784 the young American government turned to the sale of land in the Western Territory to generate necessary revenue. An effective and practical system of land measurement was required in order to facilitate the sale and ultimate settlement of the Western Territory lands. Jefferson chaired the committee tasked with the mission of identifying an appropriate method to survey and apportion the Western Territory.

The proposal presented to Congress by Jefferson's committee made use of a land grid based on a decimal system for apportionment. Jefferson proposed surveying the western lands into regular rectangular plots, with their sides running due east–west and north–south. The system ultimately adopted was easier to implement, but not as mathematically elegant. Had Congress adopted the Jefferson model, the land grid applied to the Western Territory would have been one of the first large-scale applications of a decimal-based system of measurement to be applied on a national basis.

Jefferson's proposal for surveying and allocating the western lands provides another example of his efforts to combine an important useful function with a rational, yet also elegant, set of standards. By adopting a decimal-based land surveying system, he hoped to connect land apportionment with the decimal-based system of currency he advocated. He believed that decimal-based systems were more rational and efficient. The mathematician in Jefferson also found those systems to be more attractive and aesthetically pleasing.

Also worth noting is Jefferson's involvement in the early efforts to devise and establish a fair method to apportion the number of representatives in Congress. The critical challenge faced by the Congress in 1792 was how to apportion the number of representatives allocated to each state in a manner consistent with the requirements of the Constitution. I. B. Cohen provides an excellent discussion of this challenge and Jefferson's role in resolving it.

The original allocation plan, one that was presented to President Washington by Alexander Hamilton, involved simple division of the total population of the nation by the total number of congressional seats. Thus if there were 20 total congressional seats and a population of 20,000, the calculation would yield 1,000. That figure would in turn be used to calculate the number of seats apportioned to each state. For example, if Virginia had a population of 10,000, it would be allocated 10 seats in Congress.

The calculation is more complex when the allocation does not yield a whole number. If, for instance, Virginia's population was 10,250, then the result of the allocation would equal 10.250. Under the original allocation proposal, 10.250 would be identified as the "ideal number of representatives." The actual assignment of congressional seats for Virginia, however, would not be the ideal number but would instead be 10. The actual assignment would always equal the ideal number rounded down to the nearest integral number. Of course, this rounding down would yield a total actual allocation that was less than the total ideal number of seats. As a result, a system had to be devised to allocate the extra congressional seat called for by the ideal allocation. The question to be answered was, how to award the extra congressional seat?

Three options for allocating the extra congressional seat were given serious consideration. One option was to allocate the seat to the state that had the largest total population. Another was to allocate the extra seat to the state that had the largest fractional component in its ideal number of representatives. Thus, for example, if there were two states and one had an ideal number of representatives equal to 3.456 and the other had an ideal number equal to 5.891, the extra seat would be awarded to the second state. The third option was to choose not to allocate the extra seat and simply reset the size of Congress at the actual total of congressional seats. In that case, Congress would be smaller and the fractional portions of the allocation would, in effect, be ignored.

In 1792 Congress chose to adopt the second option. The extra seat was to be awarded to the state that had the largest fractional component in the calculation for its ideal number of representatives. This approach was advocated by Alexander Hamilton. Jefferson vigorously opposed it. He opposed it, in part, because there had not been a clear public explanation of the allocation process. Jefferson insisted that the allocation system should be a clear and mathematically justifiable process that was publicly described and consistently applied. Jefferson was less open about another factor that encouraged him to oppose the allocation system. Given the population of the states at the time, the Hamilton formula favored the New England states, a result that troubled Jefferson.

Jefferson advocated a different approach to the allocation of congressional seats. He was particularly troubled that Hamilton's system allocated the extra seats based on the fractional remainders. He argued that the Constitution required that congressional seats be apportioned using a common ratio, not comparison of fractional remainders. Jefferson suggested that trial-and-error arithmetic calculations should be used to identify the largest divisor that, when divided into the population size of each state, would yield numbers (after all decimal remainders were discarded) that would sum to the chosen total size of the House of Representatives.

Jefferson's method of apportionment is commonly characterized as the "method of greatest divisors," and Jefferson was the first person in the world to propose such an allocation system. Jefferson's arguments persuaded President Washington. Washington vetoed the Hamilton proposal and supported adoption of the Jefferson allocation system. Jefferson's system was eventually enacted by Congress and remained in use for a substantial period of time.

Jefferson's profound interest in standards and his desire to craft systems of standards that were mathematically based and consistent with each other is a fascinating aspect of his personality and intellect. Also significant is his clear appreciation for the impact that technical standards have on commerce and society. Jefferson recognized that technical standards had profound economic, political, and social consequences. His efforts in a diverse range of initiatives to develop standards suggest that he appreciated the need to establish standards through methods that would foster public trust.

To that end, he was a strong proponent of open standards, requirements developed through transparent mechanisms with substantial public input. He recognized that if the public is to have faith in the integrity of standards, it must be made aware of how the standards work and how they were developed. Jefferson's appreciation of the significance of technical standards, and his sophisticated understanding of the need for transparency and a sound rational basis for those standards, anticipated the modern emphasis on setting standards.

Jefferson's work with a variety of different standards is instructive at two levels. First, it underscores the impact that technical standards have from an economic, political, and social level. Second, his work with standards illustrates his concern that all systems and processes have both a rational basis and a clear connection with practical applications. He pursued standards that were intellectually elegant yet also functionally effective and manageable. His interest in technical standards illustrates his personal connection with mathematics and his appreciation for rational, orderly processes. In part, he was intrigued by, and attracted to, challenges associated with the development of technical systems and standards because they afforded him with opportunities to apply mathematical and scientific principles for practical purposes. Just as he appreciated how Newton and others had been able to reveal the orderly processes behind the forces of nature, so too did he enjoy opportunities to establish orderly processes to govern the conduct of important human activities.

Jefferson's interest in technical standards and specifications provides another illustration of his attention both to theory and to practical impact. With regard to science, invention, and intellectual property, Jefferson consistently focused his attention on both the theoretical aspects of those activities and their applications. Technical standards is another field in which theory and practice meet. The theoretical aspect of standards primarily involves the search for a rational basis for the standards. The practical aspect involves their enforceability and the fairness of their impact. It is not surprising that different efforts to establish workable technical standards were of interest to Jefferson over the years.

His interest in technical standards provides a useful lesson for today. Government leaders should recognize, as Jefferson did, that technical standards play a vital role in the economic, political, and social life of nations. Attention to the development and implementation of those standards is an essential aspect of effective governance. That attention should be directed at both the conceptual foundations for the regulations and the practical impact of their enforcement. Care should always be exercised to ensure that the standards are devised in an open process, are based on rational assumptions, and are structured so that they can be implemented effectively.

COLLABORATIVE INVENTION FOR THE PUBLIC GOOD

Jefferson appreciated the importance of collaboration in the pursuit of knowledge and innovation. He believed that few inventions and discoveries were accomplished truly independently. Instead, he understood that advances in knowledge and improvements in practice were incremental, each advance and improvement based on generations of prior work undertaken by many different people in many different places. For Jefferson, the critical issue was not who made which advances or refinements, but what those advances and refinements could accomplish to benefit the society. His focus rested squarely on the practical applications for new knowledge and technical innovations.

Jefferson's belief in the collaborative aspects of discovery and invention was a widely shared philosophy, but it was beginning to change during Jefferson's time. As noted previously, some prominent members of the science and technology community, including Oliver Evans, and James Watt in England, ultimately adopted a strategy based on commercialization of their inventions. Many other leading inventors, including some of the most famous inventors of all time such as the Wright brothers, Henry Ford, and Samuel Morse, did the same.

The historian of science John Gribbin has noted that James Watt "was the first person to take a set of ideas from the cutting-edge of then current research in science and apply them to make a major technological advance." Gribbin contends that Watt's actions anticipated the research commercialization process now widely applied in the modern world. This formal strategy for the commercialization of scientific research, which was only emerging in the eighteenth and nineteenth centuries, relied on the development of close ties between industry and university research groups. It also placed great emphasis on intellectual property rights to support the commercialization process.

Watt was an active and aggressive user of patent law to protect his inventions. His key steam engine patent was issued in England in 1769, and between 1793 and 1799 he was heavily involved in litigation to enforce the 1769 patent. Ben Marsden estimates that Watt and his partner, Matthew Boulton, spent approximately £6,000 to pursue that litigation, which was necessary to enable Watt to maximize market opportunities for commercial distribution of his steam engine technology. Watt's strategy for both the refinement of his research and the ultimate commercialization of its results is consistent with current practice. In that sense, Watt was a pioneer of the research and commercialization process that would become prominent in later years, and that remains prominent today.

The rise of this new approach to research and technology development raised important challenges for the more open and collaborative process in which Jefferson and most of his peers had been involved. Some have characterized the Watt model for research and development as a process of industrialized research and development.

Interest in science and technology grew dramatically during the 1700s and swept across Western Europe. An important component of that interest was the allure of the commercial potential of science and technology. First in England, particularly in Birmingham and Manchester, and soon after in virtually every part of Western Europe, there was a growing recognition that scientific research could generate technology that would support commercial gain. In the 1700s the perception of a close link connecting science and technology with economic development became a widely embraced worldview. Recognition of the commercial potential of science and technology played an important role in the process of industrialization. A noteworthy portion of the world's population began to appreciate that science and technology could drive economic development through industrialization.

Jefferson was not a supporter of this drive to industrialization. Various observers repeatedly comment on Jefferson's strong preference for an agricultural-based society instead of an industrialized one. For Jefferson, agriculture offered the greatest prospect of tranquillity and pleasure for the public. Although in his later years he developed a somewhat greater tolerance for industrialization, recognizing its potential contribution to the economic strength of the nation, he never abandoned his hope that the United States would remain a predominantly agrarian society. Thus the connection associating science and technology with industrialization held little appeal for Jefferson.

However, he did appreciate another aspect of the growing social emphasis on science and technology. Francis Bacon and others recognized that science was centered on development of knowledge of nature, and that knowledge of nature was empowering for mankind. Bacon and others realized that this empowerment extended far beyond economic strength into political and social contexts as well. Science and the resulting knowledge of nature held the potential to make society more just and fair. They offered the potential to create a social order based more on merit than on birth and heritage. Individuals with no social status and no wealth could, through education and hard work, gain mastery of science, and that knowledge offered the potential for upward social mobility and notable political influence. These political and social aspects of the empowerment offered by science and technology were of great interest to Jefferson. Pursuit of knowledge by an individual could enable that individual to improve his station and life and could generate the innovations and advances that would help improve the quality of life for many others in the society as well.

Jefferson's preference for an agrarian society is not inconsistent with his strong support for science and invention. He was attracted to an agrarian lifestyle at least in part because he believed it provided the best opportunity for each person to be empowered, based on the ability of the individual to exercise control over the decisions and the activities of daily life. To be successful in agriculture, one must deal effectively with the principles and forces of nature that govern agriculture. Science was the key to understanding those natural principles and forces.

An agrarian lifestyle was not inconsistent with appreciation for science. On the contrary, scientific literacy was essential to success in that lifestyle. Jefferson's preference for an agrarian society did not suggest that he was turning away from science and innovation. Instead, that preference recognized the close ties between agriculture and both science and engineering.

During the late eighteenth and early nineteenth centuries a transition was in progress. Much of the knowledge that had been developed during the Enlightenment was being transformed into practical applications. In the earlier period, much of the emphasis of science was on understanding our natural world. During that process of exploring, investigating, and learning, collaboration was essential. As we learned more about the world and the way it functioned, people like Jefferson and his peers helped to develop useful applications for that knowledge. Many of those applications served to create a range of technologies that enabled and sustained commercial expansion. During that expansion, individuals saw opportunities to make use of the new technologies to improve their economic position. Thanks to the diffusion of knowledge and technology, some of those opportunities could be pursued by individuals acting alone. Thus in some important ways the very success of the collaborative process of science created an environment in which individuals could successfully exploit certain technologies on their own.

Jefferson fully embraced the collaborative approach to inquiry and analysis. Even though a more proprietary view of science and technology evolved during Jefferson's time, the collaborative approach to discovery and invention did not disappear. Prominent inventors such as Isambard Kingdom Brunel in England, and later Alberto Santos-Dumont working in aviation, continued to support an approach to invention and innovation that encouraged sharing of information and cooperation in development. In modern times, this tradition of collective work and cooperation emerged again in the context of open-source software and digital file sharing.

Part of the motivation driving the inventors who advocated a more open, less proprietary approach to innovation was a sense that excessive attention to patenting and assertion of proprietary control delayed the advance of innovation. Brunel, for example, believed that the focus on obtaining patent rights distracted inventors. He felt that the quest for patents kept inventors away from efforts to refine and enhance devices that were already in existence. For Brunel, the fastest route to innovation involved application of the most resourceful inventors to existing devices and products. If the most inventive people continuously reviewed the large inventory of existing devices, searching for ways to improve those devices and to apply them to new uses, Brunel believed that the benefit to society would be far greater than if inventive people focused just on creating new devices with the intent of asserting proprietary control over them. For Brunel, preoccupation with patents degraded the quality of the inventive work.

The aviator Alberto Santos-Dumont believed that aviation provided a means to improve the quality of life of the masses. For him, advances in aviation technology that made the potential benefits of aviation accessible to more people more quickly were of greatest value. Patenting advances in aviation technology did not, in his estimation, facilitate rapid public access to the latest aviation technology. Santos-Dumont had a vision of aviation technology serving to empower people, but to do so, it had to be made accessible quickly and broadly. Patents and proprietary claims impeded public access. Accordingly, Santos-Dumont chose not to patent his work, placing him in stark contrast to the Wright brothers, who adopted a highly proprietary strategy for their aviation work. While the Wright brothers worked on their aviation designs under strict secrecy in order to preserve their patent position, Santos-Dumont and other aviation pioneers worked in the open. Their development efforts involved sharing of information among a community of other aviation enthusiasts.

A prominent example of contemporary collaborative invention is the open-source process for the development of computer software. The open-source software development model is based on the concept that the software user has the best sense of how the software should be customized to suit his or her particular needs. In addition, providing more developers with access to the underlying source code facilitates more rapid improvement of the quality of the software. Open-source collaboration thus provides a faster and more economically efficient way to improve the quality of the product and to expand the range of its uses.

The open-source movement is also an appropriate modern example of some of the issues associated with invention and innovation that were of interest to Jefferson in his time. A vocal subset of the open-source movement around the world embraces a political and social philosophy that they believe is consistent with the technical and economic aspects of the open-source development process. They argue that the open-source process helps to empower individuals. It enables individual developers to modify existing products in ways of their own choosing.

The open-source model has become increasingly popular among developing countries, in Latin America and parts of Asia, for example. This popularity is driven largely by the realization that use of open-source products will give those countries a greater ability to make products that are more suitable for their specific needs and thus be less captive to designs and specifications set by large software companies. Open source provides at least a measure of independence for developing countries, making them nominally less dependent on the decisions of multinational information technology companies. The open-source process also helps developing countries to cultivate their own national community of software developers, and to encourage the growth of those communities at faster rates than the strict proprietary model would allow.

These proponents of the open-source movement support its use in the world of computer software and recognize its potential across the spectrum of technology, economics, politics, and society. They appear to embrace a philosophy similar to that expressed by Thomas Jefferson. Although one cannot assert that Jefferson would fully accept all facets of the open-source movement, it is reasonable to believe that he would appreciate the movement's sensitivity to the economic, political, and social effects of this form of technological innovation.

The open-source movement also provides a strategy for responding to concerns that proprietary intellectual property rights may ultimately choke off innovation. Some fear that the rise in popularity of patents for computer programs could seriously impede innovation by blocking access to proprietary computer code for software researchers and developers. When patents are obtained for computer programs, they can be enforced against other programs that, though not identical to the patented version, may be substantially similar to it.

One response to concern about the broad use of software patents is to actively encourage widespread disclosure of computer code as it is developed. To obtain a patent for a computer program, the applicant must demonstrate that the code involved is novel and nonobvious. It becomes increasingly difficult to make such a showing effectively in an environment in which a large volume of computer code has already been disclosed. The open-source community provides a nearly perfect vehicle for this strategy. The more code that is disclosed through the open-source process, the more difficult it will be for a developer to satisfy the novelty and nonobviousness requirements.

In this way, an active and expansive open-source software community will likely reduce the effectiveness of software patenting strategies. This open-source strategy makes it more difficult to establish proprietary control over computer code and offers an approach to the challenge that might well have appealed to Jefferson. The strategy, in effect, uses knowledge dissemination to overwhelm efforts to establish proprietary control over intellectual property. By sharing new knowledge rapidly and broadly, the community can make it more difficult for anyone to assert proprietary control over the knowledge. Through this process, the community essentially outpaces the ability of any single individual to move quickly enough to establish an exclusive proprietary interest. A community of many software developers modifying and enhancing the original open-source programs can create a significant volume of prior art quickly enough to make it noticeably more difficult for proprietary software developers to create code that is novel and nonobvious.

A lesson we can take from Jefferson is the recognition that additions to the collective knowledge base and widespread access to innovations benefit society even in those instances where there is no single, dominant owner of core intellectual property. In our modern environment we tend to equate success in innovation with the existence of a single dominant new product. The absence of a dominant technology provider is often interpreted as a sign of limited innovation or failure of strategic vision. We tend to glorify instances when a single inventor has developed a breakthrough advance. Although those instances are extremely rare, we have grown accustomed to attaching a single person or company to a successful innovation and glorifying that individual, even when there were actually many different people and organizations that made important contributions to the breakthrough.

An example of this modern tendency comes from the emergence of personal computing technology. Much has been written about the fact that many of the key technologies associated with the rise of personal computers and computer networking were developed in the innovative and successful research laboratory of Xerox Corporation, the Xerox Palo Alto Research Center, or PARC. Xerox has been widely criticized for largely failing to commercially exploit many of the core computing technologies that its researchers developed. Far less has been written about the fact that although Xerox was not the company that took many of these technologies to market, the technologies ultimately did get to the market, and succeeded dramatically.

The world has been substantially changed, and improved, by the technologies developed by PARC. Although Xerox's failure to play the leading role in that commercialization could be seen as a negative by the company, it is not a negative from the perspective of society as a whole. From that broader perspective, it does not matter who brings innovations to the society. All that matters is that those innovations get to as many people as possible as quickly as possible.

Jefferson recognized this distinction. His focus was always on the need to promote innovation and to facilitate its rapid diffusion throughout society. He recognized that intellectual property rights had a role to play in promoting that diffusion, and he appreciated their value to the extent that they helped to encourage integration of inventions and new works into useful applications. When intellectual property rights were applied in ways that interfered with that integration, however, Jefferson consistently sided with the need to promote integration over the enforcement of the proprietary rights.

When emphasis is placed on a broader public purpose for invention, there is a greater readiness to promote collaboration and openness in the inventive process. The proprietary model of invention and development is a far more closed model. In part, it must be closed, since patent law generally requires that an inventor seeking to establish patent rights must demonstrate that his work is novel, not present in the prior art. Disclosure of the invention in advance of patenting undermines the inventor's ultimate ability to obtain a patent. The decision to pursue patent rights essentially requires adoption of a closed research and development model. As greater emphasis is placed on establishing proprietary intellectual property rights, the open, collaborative environment for research is gradually lost.

Today we see other examples of the tension between assertion of proprietary rights for intellectual property and adoption of a more open, collaborative strategy. In recent years many research universities have placed a high priority on trying to derive maximum economic return from the inventions they developed. The results of those efforts have been mixed. A relatively few universities have made significant amounts of money, in most cases from a handful of extremely successful inventions, but the majority of them have earned relatively little. Now, some universities are re-examining their objectives. There is growing interest among universities in emphasizing the public benefits that can be derived from their research and inventions. Those universities are beginning to adopt commercialization strategies that seek to move their technologies as quickly as possible into applications that offer the potential for the greatest public benefit. It is reasonable to believe that Jefferson would applaud this shift in priorities.

Preservation of the openness and communication necessary for collaborative research and innovation was an important goal of Jefferson's. By placing the greatest priority on rapid transformation of new knowledge to useful practical applications, he emphasized the importance of collaboration. He believed that a community of knowledgeable individuals could be far more successful at obtaining new knowledge and engaging that knowledge to meet society's needs quickly than could any single individual. We would be well served to appreciate that perspective in our modern age.

SCIENCE, TECHNOLOGY, AND POLITICAL LEADERSHIP

Jefferson and his generation of American political leaders offer insights into the potential power of political leaders as promoters of open inquiry, invention and innovation, and dissemination of knowledge. As we have previously discussed, America has not had a generation of political leaders with the same appreciation for, and understanding of, the economic, political, and social significance of the quest for new knowledge and the rapid widespread dissemination of that knowledge since Jefferson's time. Although we recognize that the Enlightenment-era connection between political leaders and intellectual leaders led to remarkable advances in that age, we have not seriously attempted to promote similar connections in our own time. Perhaps it is time to foster such connections in a more organized and systematic way.

The point is not that political leaders should be world-class scientists. Demanding that those leaders attain elite status in the world of science, as Franklin did, is both unreasonable and unnecessary. Instead, what would be both helpful and reasonable is the expectation that political leaders be scientifically literate and that they establish and maintain a connection with the world of science and technology through at least a basic level of direct experience. Jefferson and his colleagues provide a model for the value of the scientist/statesman.

It is unreasonable to expect that our political leaders will achieve world-class status as professionals in science or technology. It is reasonable to expect that they will cultivate a sense of curiosity regarding the current status and future potential in a range of scientific and technological disciplines. It is reasonable to expect that they will attain a level of fluency in scientific principles and concepts that will enable them to understand and appreciate the basic challenges and advances associated with a range of scientific fields. Finally, it is also reasonable to expect that they will maintain at least a basic level of direct connection with advances in science and technology. This connection should involve more than briefings and photo opportunities. It should involve direct interaction with scientists and new technology. Political leaders should be active users of new technology and interested participants in the scientific advances continually taking place around them.

At a minimum, we should begin to expect that political leaders avoid embracing philosophies and policies that are based on unsound scientific principles or obviously flawed analytical processes. For example, much attention has been paid in the United States to educational curricula in the public schools, particularly with regard to the subject of biological evolution. Some school systems took the position that evolution should not be taught as scientific fact, but should instead be included as one of several "theories" explaining the creation and development of life on earth. They acted to ensure that other theories — intelligent design, for example — would also be taught as alternatives to the Darwinian model of evolution.

Many political leaders actively supported the movement to add intelligent design to the curriculum of the biological sciences in the public schools. They took this position in spite of active and widespread advocacy by the scientific community, which argued that those alternative theories of evolution did not constitute sound scientific work. This is a public issue that could have benefited substantially from involvement by political leaders who, regardless of political affiliation and philosophy, possessed a more thorough understanding of science and the scientific method and were driven by greater respect for the significance of science. Instead of appealing to the scientific misconceptions of the public, our political leaders must be prepared and willing to help citizens achieve a more accurate and complete understanding of the ways in which science and technology influence our daily lives.

Jefferson's experience provides an example of how such political leadership could be exerted. Jefferson wrote his book *Notes on the State of Virginia* at least in part to correct scientific misconceptions about the American continent that were widely accepted in Europe, even among the more educated and ruling elites. Admittedly, the European misconceptions addressed by Jefferson largely supported a perception of European superiority over all things American, and so his book was also partially motivated by political goals. Yet it is also true that Jefferson wrote in an effort to correct factual inaccuracies and to enlighten and inform the public. Jefferson recognized that part of the function of political leaders is to help to educate the public.

To advocate more active connections between political leaders of today and the world of science and technology is not to claim that Jefferson and his colleagues were above using their knowledge in support of partisan political purposes. They were practicing politicians, and they commonly applied their knowledge and scientific connections in support of partisan goals. Nor does this argument suggest that Jefferson and his peers were always correct with respect to their scientific knowledge.

They were, however, literate with respect to the science and technology of their time. They were active members of the leading science and technology knowledge networks. Through those networks they kept informed of the most current advances, and they tested their ideas and plans. In short, they were informed about science and technology, interested in those fields, and actively engaged in them. Each generation should be able to expect at least as much from its political leaders.

Jefferson's long association with the leading knowledge networks of his time, and his active use of those networks as a resource, offer a particularly helpful lesson for today. Jefferson's connection to those knowledge networks was important to him personally, but it was also a valuable asset for the United States. Jefferson was a better political leader because he was connected to many of the other intellectual leaders of his time. Similar connections can be of great value for our country today as well.

It is not necessary that our political leaders be the most intelligent people in the society. It is important, however, that they are connected to knowledge networks that can help them to understand the critical issues of the day and to formulate effective strategies and policies to address those issues successfully. Jefferson's example illustrates how important and productive those networks and connections can be.

Jefferson and his colleagues consistently tried to apply the most current knowledge of the day to the policy challenges they faced. They made use of scientific methods to identify, analyze, and address the problems faced by the nation. Although this approach did not always yield the most effective response, it did provide a measure of rationality to the process of governance. Application of a rational analytical process to the activities of governance encourages greater public confidence in government's integrity and effectiveness. The Founding Fathers believed in the effectiveness of the rational method, and they applied it, as best they could, in all facets of their activities, including public governance. Modern political leaders could benefit from similar efforts.

All too often in our time, there is a perception that political leaders develop and implement policy based, not on rational analysis of data and options, but instead on ideology. Many believe that desired policy objectives are established first, then data are manufactured to justify the policy. Healthy respect for the value of a more objective and rigorous process of defining problems and developing policy by political leaders can lead to more effective policy choices and greater confidence in the integrity of the government on the part of the public.

FINAL THOUGHTS

Thomas Jefferson developed and applied a philosophy regarding intellectual property rights that was comprehensive and very much a product of his time. He understood that intellectual property rights do not stand in isolation but are connected to the principle of widespread dissemination of information and knowledge. Those rights are linked to public education and to economic development. Jefferson understood that policies regarding science, education, access to information, and intellectual property carry profound economic, political, and social consequences. Although his vision of intellectual property was shaped by the values of the Enlightenment, there are lessons from that vision that are appropriate for our time as well.

Jefferson understood that intellectual property rights are not final objectives but tools intended to advance broader objectives. Nor are they policy tools to be used in isolation. Instead, they are to be used in conjunction with policies that address education, research, communication, and innovation. Our objective is not to maximize the number of patents issued or even to maximize the amount of money generated by the inventions those patents represent. Instead, our objective is to structure and enforce intellectual property rights in such ways that those rights help to encourage the extension of knowledge and the rapid, widespread dissemination of that knowledge, along with prompt translation of new knowledge into applications that improve the quality of life for all members of the society.

Knowledge, invention, and innovation must be used to find practical solutions to human needs. Intellectual property rights are one of many tools that can effectively cultivate an economic, political, and social environment conducive to rapid and continuing application of knowledge, invention, and innovation to enhance the quality of life. Intellectual property rights are one tool, not the only tool, and, perhaps more important, they are not the policy goal.

Intellectual property can provide a source of empowerment. It empowers individuals by providing them with the tools necessary to be self-reliant, yet also effective participants in their community. It empowers the society by providing the resources that helps the society become more just and humane. Perhaps most important, Jefferson and his peers imagined a society in which everyone, rich and poor alike, would have access to the benefits associated with the common pool of knowledge developed by mankind over the generations. The economic, political, and social advantages derived from application of the sum total of the society's knowledge would be used for the benefit of the society as a whole. As the knowledge base grew, the benefits to the entire society would also grow. For Jefferson, information, investigation, and communication generated knowledge. Knowledge was shared through education. Knowledge combined with incentives and inventiveness created applications that improved the quality of life. All of these key concepts were intricately linked. Jefferson recognized those connections and acted accordingly. This holistic vision of the essential links connecting information, knowledge, communication, intellectual property, and innovation was an integral part of his view of the world. It is this vision that will prove to be most helpful for us as we address the challenges of the future.

Instead of using extensive footnotes, in this section I provide a summary of the source materials used, by chapter, to assist interested readers. All works cited here are included in the bibliography.

1. INTELLECTUAL PROPERTY RIGHTS TODAY

Informative discussions of the development and the evolution of the open-source software movement are available in the books by Moody (2002) and Wayner (2000). Evolving notions of the value of information in a networked environment are addressed in Levine et al. (2000). Background on the development of the Internet and its implications can be found in Hafner and Lyon (1996). The challenge of valuing and managing commercial development of intellectual property is addressed by Rivette and Kline (2000). Examination of alternatives to intellectual property law that may more effectively balance the interests of creative content developers and users is provided by Thierer and Crews (2002).

Hindle and Lubar (1986) offer insight into the substantial and significant flow of technical expertise from Europe to the United States in the early years of American development. Helpful discussion of Jefferson's appreciation of the need to monitor scientific and technological advances in Europe for the future benefit of the United States is provided by Malone (1951, 2:83). Jefferson's 1788 letter to Rutledge identifying technological "Objects of Attention for an American" in Europe is in Boyd (1950–, 13:269). Discussion of the willingness of Alexander Hamilton and other early American political leaders to encourage and support technology piracy in the name of U.S. economic development is available in Ben-Atar (2004).

Marsden (2002, 137) offers interesting background on Watt's struggles to protect his proprietary steam engine technology. This discussion shows that Watt was among the first to recognize and adopt the modern concept of technology commercialization.

Gribbin (2002) gives a helpful historical review of the evolution of science and offers an excellent overview of the rise of modern science. Khan (2005) presents useful information on the development of American patent and copyright law, and their relation to the nation's economic development.

2. JEFFERSON AND THE VALUE OF SHARED KNOWLEDGE

Jefferson's "A Bill for the More General Diffusion of Knowledge" is available in Peterson (1984, 365). His 1786 letter to George Wythe can be found in

Boyd (1950–, 10:244). Baker (1975) offers a helpful examination of Condorcet's philosophy. The 1813 letter to Isaac McPherson is in Peterson (1984, 1286). Discussion of Jefferson's comprehensive interest in education at all levels is provided by Malone (1981, 6:233).

Jefferson's discussion of the openness of the community of science even during time of war, in the context of the information on plow technology, is available in his 1809 letter to John Hollins, in Peterson (1984, 1200).

Jefferson discusses his plans for the University of Virginia in his 1800 letter to Joseph Priestley, in Peterson (1984, 1069). Additional discussion of his role in the creation of the University of Virginia is presented by Malone (1981, 6:411). His involvement in the development of West Point is addressed by McDonald (2004) and Malone (1974, 5:510).

Comment on Jefferson and exploration is available in Ambrose (1996) and Goetzmann (1966). Helpful material is also provided by Jackson (1962). See Malone (1974, 5:174) for a discussion of Jefferson's insistence that Lewis and Clark be prepared to make scientific observations during their expedition. The instructions for the expedition issued by Jefferson are included in his letter to Lewis, in Peterson (1984, 1126). Malone (1974, 5:207) addresses Jefferson's pleasure with the scientific results of the expedition and his eagerness to share them.

Jefferson's 1799 letter to William Green Mumford discussing the perpetual nature of knowledge once expressed and the importance of knowledge sharing for the improvement of man is in Peterson (1984, 1063).

3. KINDRED SPIRIT TO SCIENTISTS AND INVENTORS

Cohen (1995) offers an excellent discussion of the role science played in influencing the political thought of Jefferson, Adams, Franklin, and Madison. Cohen (1995) also refers to Theodore Roosevelt's expertise as a natural scientist. Jefferson's 1809 letter to Du Pont de Nemours is in Peterson (1984, 1203). His 1800 letter to Martha Jefferson Randolph is in Boyd (1950–, 31:365). Cohen (1995) discusses Franklin's global fame as a scientist in the field of electricity. An overview of Jefferson's work in paleontology involving the Megalonyx is in Cohen (1995, 290). Jefferson's paper on the Megalonyx fossil find, "Memoir on the Meglonyx," is in Boyd (1950–, 29:291). Jefferson's *Notes on the State of Virginia* is in Peterson (1984, 123); his references to the special scientific expertise of Franklin and Rittenhouse are on 190. Reference to Thomas Paine's active interest in iron bridge design is in Brown (2001, 48, 49, 76). The impact of efforts to observe the 1761 and 1769 transits of Venus is discussed by Wills (1978, 111).

The impact of Enlightenment values on Jefferson and the Founding Fathers is addressed by Wills (1978). Jefferson's efforts to apply Newton's principles regarding the forces of nature to human conduct ("the human machinery") are also discussed by Wills (1978, 95). Broader examination of Newton's impact on society is in Feingold (2004).

The special skills of Alexander von Humboldt are discussed by Helferich (2004). The noted polymath Thomas Young is profiled by Robinson (2006). Malone (1962, 3:345) provides a quotation from Harlow Shapley on Jefferson's special skills as a scientist. Jefferson's work to promote public health use of vaccinations is examined by Malone (1970, 4:185). Discussion of the challenges associated with early American initiatives in vaccinations and other public health efforts is found in Brodsky (2004) and Pickstone (2001).

Jefferson's respect for Bacon, Newton, and Locke is expressed in his 1789 letter to John Trumbull, in Peterson (1984, 939). Jefferson's 1778 letter to David Rittenhouse is presented in Peterson (1984, 762). The recognition of Rittenhouse as America's leading "mechanic" is in Wills (1978, 100), as is Jefferson's admiration for Rittenhouse as a self-taught man of science (1978, 101). Additional insight into Rittenhouse is offered by Hindle (1964). Jefferson's relationship with his intellectual mentors Small, Fauquier, and Wythe is discussed by Malone (1948, 1:102). The importance of the Lunar Society is reviewed by Uglow (2002) and Schofield (1963). Discussion of Jefferson as a scientist is presented by Bedini (1990), Martin (1952), and Browne (1944).

Jefferson's 1789 letter to Joseph Willard is provided in Peterson (1984, 947). The 1787 letter from Jefferson to Jeudy de l'Hommande can be found in Boyd (1950–, 12:11). The 1794 letter from Jefferson to Richard Morris is also in Boyd (28:106).

Helpful discussion of Jefferson's inventive work with the cipher wheel is available in Bedini (1990). Discussion of the plow moldboard technology is provided by Wills (1978, 100) and Cohen (1995, 293). Examination of Jefferson's work as an inventor involved with the polygraph and other devices is in Bedini (1984).

Jefferson's passion for architecture is examined by Malone (1948, 1:144), and his love of mathematics is outlined on 1:54.

Jefferson's 1807 letter to Robert Fulton is in Peterson (1984, 1185). His 1810 letter to Fulton is quoted by Pursell (2001, 21). His 1797 letter to John Oliver is in Boyd (1950–, 29:408).

Jefferson's 1791 "Report on Desalination of Seawater" to the U.S. Congress, which provides his review of the Jacobs Isaacks desalination system, is available in Boyd (1950–, 22:318). Also of interest on the Isaacks matter are Isaacks's 1791 letter to Jefferson (Boyd 1950–, 19:1974) and Jefferson's 1791 letter to Isaacks (Boyd 1950–, 19:623). Jefferson's love of science and invention is discussed by Malone (1970, 4:180).

4. THE FIRST PATENT EXAMINER

A discussion of C. C. Pinckney's role in the development of the intellectual property rights portion of the Constitution is in Cohen (1995, 239–40). Cohen (1995, 241–43) also offers a helpful analysis of the differences between the constitutional provisions supporting promotion of science and the useful arts, and providing exclusive rights to authors and inventors. Dray (2005) presents an interesting examination of Franklin's work with the lightning rod and its connections with his basic research in the field of electricity.

Helpful material on the history of copyright and patent law in the United States is provided by Bugbee (1967). Also helpful are Walterscheid (1998) and Vojacek (1936). Dutton (1984) offers a valuable overview of the relationship between patent law and the development of the innovations that drove the Industrial Revolution.

Jefferson's 1792 letter to Hugh Williamson describing his concerns over the burdens associated with the patent review process is in Boyd (1950–, 23:363). His 1791 draft of proposals for revisions to the Patent Act, "A Bill to Promote the Progress of the Useful Arts" is also in Boyd (1950–, 22:359). Jefferson's 1788 letter to James Madison outlining his concerns regarding monopolies is in Boyd (1950–, 13:442), as is his 1790 letter to Benjamin Vaughan (16:578).

Jefferson's 1813 letter to Isaac McPherson discussing ownership rights for ideas and inventions is in Peterson (1984, 1286).

Dutton (1984) provides an effective discussion of the relationship between the patent system and invention in England during the Industrial Revolution. He examines the connection between patents and economic incentive for development of commercial applications for technology.

5. JEFFERSON BATTLES THE PATENT TROLLS

Additional information on Oliver Evans is provided by Bathe and Bathe (1935) and Ferguson (1980). Hunter (1979, 430) provides a strong endorsement of the technical value of the Evans milling technology. Jefferson details his objections to the Evans patent in his 1813 letter to Isaac McPherson, in Peterson (1984, 1286).

6. JEFFERSON AND THE CHALLENGES
OF INVENTION AND INNOVATION

Jefferson's comments on the importance of science to society and the need to access foreign sources of science is quoted by Bedini (1990, 373). The 1785 letter from Jefferson to Bellini is in Peterson (1984, 832), as is his 1807 letter to Wistar (1181), and his 1787 letter to de Crèvecoeur (877). Jefferson's concern for Priestley is examined by Malone (1962, 3:386).

Jefferson's 1791 "Report on Weights and Measures" for the U.S. Congress is available in Boyd (1950–, 16:602). Wills (1978, 105) addresses Jefferson's desire to create a new approach to standards of measurement for America. The comments on the complexity of Jefferson's description of his proposed standards of measurement are in Cohen (1995, 108). Jefferson's role in the development of standardized currency is discussed by Linklater (2003, 65–66), who also offers a helpful examination of Jefferson's proposals regarding a decimal-based system for allocating American public lands. Cohen (1995, 90) provides an overview of Jefferson's approach to the problem of developing a fair process for allocation of congressional seats.

Gribbin (2002, 249) presents a clear review of James Watt's position as one of the first inventors to work closely, in a systematic way, with ongoing work at research institutions. Marsden (2002, 138–46) provides an examination of Watt's active patent strategy and the way that strategy was integrated into a commercialization plan. Jacob and Stewart (2004) offer a helpful overview of the process through which public acceptance of science helped to drive the development of technology and the movement to industrialization in Europe and America. Mokyr (1990 and 2002) presents helpful analysis of the role of science and technology in industrialization and economic growth. Malone (1981, 6:85, 146–47) describes Jefferson's preference for an agrarian society, which remained with him throughout his life, although as he aged he seemed to acknowledge more clearly that industry had a role to play in economic development. The tension between collaborative development and proprietary efforts in the early aviation industry is addressed by Hoffman (2003), Shulman (2002), and Tobin (2003). Discussion of the efforts of the Xerox PARC enterprise is presented by Smith and Alexander (1988) and Hiltzik (1999).

SELECTED BIBLIOGRAPHY

Adams, William Howard. 1997. *The Paris Years of Thomas Jefferson.* New Haven: Yale University Press.

Ambrose, Stephen E. 1996. *Undaunted Courage: Meriwether Lewis, Thomas Jefferson, and the Opening of the American West.* New York: Simon and Schuster.

Auerbach, Jeffrey A. 1999. *The Great Exhibition of 1851: A Nation on Display.* New Haven: Yale University Press.

Baker, Keith Michael. 1975. *Condorcet: From Natural Philosophy to Social Mathematics.* Chicago: University of Chicago Press.

Bathe, Greville, and Dorothy Bathe. 1935. *Oliver Evans: A Chronicle of Early American Engineering.* Philadelphia: Historical Society of Pennsylvania.

Bedini, Silvio A. 1984. *Thomas Jefferson and His Copying Machines.* Charlottesville: University of Virginia Press.

———. *Thomas Jefferson: Statesman of Science.* 1990. New York: Macmillan.

Bell, Whitfield J. 1955. *Early American Science: Needs and Opportunities.* Williamsburg: Institute of Early American History and Culture.

Ben-Atar, Doron S. 2004. *Trade Secrets: Intellectual Piracy and the Origins of American Industrial Power.* New Haven: Yale University Press.

Betts, Edwin M., ed. 1953. *Thomas Jefferson's Farm Book with Commentary and Relevant Extracts from Other Writings.* Princeton: Princeton University Press.

Boorstin, Daniel. 1948. *The Lost World of Thomas Jefferson.* Boston: Beacon Press.

Boyd, Julian P., ed. 1950–. *The Papers of Thomas Jefferson.* Princeton: Princeton University Press.

Brodsky, Alyn. 2004. *Benjamin Rush: Patriot and Physician.* New York: St. Martin's Press.

Brown, David J. 2001. *Bridges: Three Thousand Years of Defying Nature.* St. Paul, Minn.: MBI Publishing.

Browne, Charles A. 1944. *Thomas Jefferson and the Scientific Trends of His Time.* Waltham, Mass.: Chronica Botanica Company.

Bugbee, Bruce. 1967. *The Genesis of American Patent and Copyright Law.* Washington, D.C.: Public Affairs Press.

Carlson, Bernard W. 1991. *Innovation as a Social Process: Elihu Thomson and the Rise of General Electric, 1870–1900.* New York: Cambridge University Press.

Carter, Edward C., ed. 1988. *The Papers of Benjamin Henry Latrobe*. New Haven: Yale University Press.

Cohen, I. Bernard, ed. 1980. *Thomas Jefferson and the Sciences*. New York: Arno Press.

———. 1990. *Benjamin Franklin's Science*. Cambridge, Mass.: Harvard University Press.

———. 1995. *Science and the Founding Fathers*. New York: W. W. Norton.

Crowther, J. G. 1960. *Founders of British Science*. London: Cresset Press.

———. 1962. *Scientists of the Industrial Revolution*. London: Cresset Press.

Desmond, Adrian, and James Moore. 1991. *Darwin*. New York: Warner Books.

Dorfman, Joseph. 1946. *The Economic Mind in American Civilization, 1606–1865*. New York: Viking.

Dray, Philip. 2005. *Stealing God's Thunder: Benjamin Franklin's Lightning Rod and the Invention of America*. New York: Random House.

Dutton, H. I. 1984. *The Patent System and Inventive Activity during the Industrial Revolution: 1750–1852*. Manchester: Manchester University Press.

Ellis, Joseph J. 1996. *American Sphinx: The Character of Thomas Jefferson*. New York: Vintage Books.

Feingold, Mordechai. 2004. *The Newtonian Moment: Isaac Newton and the Making of Modern Culture*. New York: Oxford University Press.

Ferguson, Eugene S. 1980. *Oliver Evans: Inventive Genius of the American Industrial Revolution*. Greenville, Del.: Hagley Museum.

———. *Engineering and the Mind's Eye*. 1992. Cambridge, Mass.: MIT Press.

Ford, Paul Leicester, ed. 1892–1899. *The Writings of Thomas Jefferson*. 10 vols. New York: G. P. Putnam's Sons.

Gilbreath, James. 1999. *Thomas Jefferson and the Education of a Citizen*. Washington, D.C.: Library of Congress.

Goetzmann, William H. 1966. *Exploration and Empire*. New York: History Book Club.

Golinski, Jan. 1992. *Science as Public Culture: Chemistry and Enlightenment in Britain, 1760–1820*. Cambridge: Cambridge University Press.

Greene, John C. 1984. *American Science in the Age of Jefferson*. Ames: Iowa State University Press.

Gribbin, John. 2002. *Science: A History 1543–2001*. New York: Penguin Press.

Hafner, Katie, and Matthew Lyon. 1996. *Where Wizards Stay Up Late: The Origins of the Internet*. New York: Simon and Schuster.

Halliday, E. M. 2001. *Understanding Thomas Jefferson*. New York: HarperCollins.

Harris, C. M., ed. 1995–. *Papers of William Thornton*. Charlottesville: University Press of Virginia.

Hawke, David Freeman. 1976. *Franklin*. New York: Harper and Row.

Helferich, Gerard. 2004. *Humboldt's Cosmos*. New York: Gotham Books.

Hellenbrand, Harold. 1990. *The Unfinished Revolution: Education and Politics in the Thought of Thomas Jefferson*. Newark: University of Delaware Press.

Hiltzik, Michael. 1999. *Dealers of Lightning*. New York: HarperCollins.

Hindle, Brooke. 1956. *The Pursuit of Science in Revolutionary America, 1735–1789*. Chapel Hill: University of North Carolina Press.

———. 1964. *David Rittenhouse*. Princeton: Princeton University Press.

———. 1981. *Emulation and Invention*. New York: New York University Press.

Hindle, Brooke, and Steven Lubar. 1986. *Engines of Change*. Washington, D.C.: Smithsonian Institution Press.

Hoffman, Paul. 2003. *Wings of Madness: Alberto Santos-Dumont and the Invention of Flight*. New York: Hyperion.

Honeywell, Ray J. 1931. *The Educational Work of Thomas Jefferson*. Cambridge, Mass.: Harvard University Press.

Hippel, Eric von. 1988. *The Sources of Innovation*. New York: Oxford University Press.

Hunt, Gaillard, and James Brown Scott, eds. 1987. *Debates in the Federal Convention of 1787*. Buffalo: Prometheus Books.

Hunter, Louis C. 1979. *Waterpower in the Century of the Steam Engine*. Charlottesville: University Press of Virginia.

Jackson, Donald, ed. 1962. *The Letters of the Lewis and Clark Expedition with Related Documents, 1783–1854*. Urbana: University of Illinois Press.

Jacob, Margaret C., and Larry Stewart. 2004. *Practical Matters: Newton's Science in the Service of Industry and Empire*. Cambridge, Mass.: Harvard University Press.

Jardine, Lisa. 1999. *Ingenious Pursuits: Building the Scientific Revolution*. New York: Anchor Books.

Khan, B. Zorina. 2005. *The Democratization of Invention: Patent and Copyrights in American Economic Development*. New York: Cambridge University Press.

Koch, Adrienne. 1943. *The Philosophy of Thomas Jefferson*. New York: Columbia University Press.

Landes, Davis S. 1998. *The Wealth and Poverty of Nations*. New York: Norton.

Lehmann, Karl. 1965. *Thomas Jefferson, American Humanist*. Chicago: University of Chicago Press.

Levine, Rick, et al. 2000. *The Cluetrain Manifesto: The End of Business as Usual*. Cambridge, Mass.: Perseus Books.

Lindley, David. 2004. *Degrees Kelvin*. Washington, D.C.: John Henry Press.

Linklater, Andro. 2003. *Measuring America*. New York: Penguin Group.

Lipscomb, A. A., and A. E. Bergh, eds. 1903–4. *The Writings of Thomas Jefferson*. 20 vols. Washington, D.C.

Malone, Dumas. 1948. *Jefferson the Virginian*. Vol. 1 of *Jefferson and His Time*. Boston: Little, Brown.

———. 1951. *Jefferson and the Rights of Man*. Vol. 2 of *Jefferson and His Time*. Boston: Little, Brown.

———. 1962. *Jefferson and the Ordeal of Liberty*. Vol. 3 of *Jefferson and His Time*. Boston: Little, Brown.

———. 1970. *Jefferson the President: First Term, 1801–1805*. Vol. 4 of *Jefferson and His Time*. Boston: Little, Brown.

———. 1974. *Jefferson the President: Second Term, 1805–1809*. Vol. 5 of *Jefferson and His Time*. Boston: Little, Brown.

———. 1981. *The Sage of Monticello*. Vol. 6 of *Jefferson and His Time*. Boston: Little, Brown.

Marsden, Ben. 2002. *Watt's Perfect Engine*. London: Icon Books.

Martin, Edwin T. 1952. *Thomas Jefferson: Scientist*. New York: Henry Schuman.

Mason, Stephen F. 1962. *A History of the Sciences*. New York: Macmillan.

Mayer, David N. 1994. *The Constitutional Thought of Thomas Jefferson*. Charlottesville: University Press of Virginia.

McClellan, James E., III. 1985. *Science Recognized: Scientific Societies in the Eighteenth Century*. New York: Columbia University Press.

McDonald, Robert M. S., ed. 2004. *Thomas Jefferson's Military Academy*. Charlottesville: University of Virginia Press.

McGraw, Judith A. 1994. *Early American Technology*. Chapel Hill: University of North Carolina Press.

Miller, Charles A. 1988. *Jefferson and Nature: An Interpretation*. Baltimore: Johns Hopkins University Press.

Miller, Lillian B., ed. 1988. *The Selected Papers of Charles Willson Peale*. New Haven: Yale University Press.

Miller, Nathan. 1992. *Theodore Roosevelt: A Life*. New York: William Morrow.

Mokyr, Joel. 1990. *The Lever of Riches: Technological Creativity and Economic Growth*. New York: Oxford University Press.

———. 2002. *The Gifts of Athena: Historical Origins of the Knowledge Economy*. Princeton: Princeton University Press.

Moody, Glyn. 2002. *Rebel Code: The Inside Story of Linux and the Open Source Revolution*. Cambridge, Mass.: Perseus Publishing.

Mowery, David, and Nathan Rosenberg. 1989. *Technology and the Pursuit of Economic Growth*. Cambridge: Cambridge University Press.

Musson, A. E., and Eric Robinson. 1969. *Science and Technology in the Industrial Revolution.* Toronto: University of Toronto Press.

O'Brian, Patrick. 1993. *Joseph Banks: A Life.* Boston: David R. Godine.

Pancaldi, Giuliano. 2003. *Volta: Science and Culture in the Age of Enlightenment.* Princeton: Princeton University Press.

Peterson, Merrill D. 1970. *Thomas Jefferson and the New Nation.* New York: Oxford University Press.

———, ed. 1984. *Writings, Thomas Jefferson.* Library of America, 17. New York: Literary Classics of the United States.

Pickstone, John V. 2001. *Ways of Knowing: A New History of Science, Technology, and Medicine.* Chicago: University of Chicago Press.

Pursell, Carroll W., Jr. 1995. *The Machine in America: A Social History of Technology.* Baltimore: Johns Hopkins University Press.

———, ed. 2001. *Technology in America.* 2nd ed. Cambridge, Mass.: MIT Press.

Riskin, Jessica. 2002. *Science in the Age of Sensibility: The Sentimental Empiricists of the French Enlightenment.* Chicago: University of Chicago Press.

Rivette, Kevin G., and David Kline. 2000. *Rembrandts in the Attic.* Boston: Harvard Business School Press.

Robinson, Andrew. 2006. *The Last Man Who Knew Everything.* New York: Pi Press.

Rosenberg, Nathan, Ralph Landau, and David C. Mowery, eds. 1992. *Technology and the Wealth of Nations.* Stanford: Stanford University Press.

Saricks, Ambrose. 1965. *Pierre Samuel du Pont de Nemours.* Lawrence: University of Kansas Press.

Schofield, Robert E. 1963. *The Lunar Society of Birmingham: A Social History of Provincial Science and Industry in Eighteenth-Century England.* Oxford: Clarendon Press.

Shapin, Steven. 1966. *The Scientific Revolution.* Chicago: University of Chicago Press.

Sheldon, Garrett Ward. 1991. *The Political Philosophy of Thomas Jefferson.* Baltimore: Johns Hopkins University Press.

Shulman, Seth. 2002. *Unlocking the Sky: Glenn Hammond Curtis and the Race to Invent the Airplane.* New York: HarperCollins.

Silverman, Kenneth. 2003. *Lightning Man: The Accursed Life of Samuel F. B. Morse.* Cambridge, Mass.: Da Capo Press.

Smith, Douglas K., and Robert C. Alexander. 1988. *Fumbling the Future.* New York: William Morrow.

Smith, James Morton, ed. 1995. *The Republic of Letters: The Correspondence between Thomas Jefferson and James Madison, 1776–1826.* 3 vols. New York: W. W. Norton.

Sobol, Dana. 1995. *Longitude.* New York: Penguin Books.

Stewart, Larry. 2001. *The Rise of Public Science.* Cambridge: Cambridge University Press.

Stewart, Matthew. 2006. *The Courtier and the Heretic.* New York: W. W. Norton.

Thierer, Adam, and Wayne Crews Jr., eds. 2002. *Copy Fights.* Washington, D.C.: Cato Institute.

Tobin, James. 2003. *To Conquer the Air.* New York: Free Press.

Uglow, Jenny. 2002. *The Lunar Men.* New York: Farrar, Straus and Giroux.

Vojacek, Jan. 1936. *A Survey of the Principal National Patent Systems.* New York: Prentice-Hall.

Walterscheid, Edward C. 1998. *To Promote the Progress of Useful Arts: American Patent Law and Administration, 1798–1836.* Littleton, Colo.: Fred B. Rothman.

Wayner, Peter. 2000. *Free for All.* New York: HarperBusiness.

Wills, Gary. 1978. *Inventing America.* Garden City: Doubleday.

Wolf, A. A. 1938. *A History of Science, Technology, and Philosophy in the Eighteenth Century.* London: George Allen.

INDEX

Federalist, essays by Madison, 57
file sharing, 14
Ford, Henry, 124
fossils, 55
Franklin, Benjamin, 46, 54, 55, 57,
   81, 133
freedom of scientific inquiry, 64–65
French Academy of Sciences, 58
French encyclopedists, 38
Fulton, Robert, 69

Garriga, José, 55
geology, 45, 48, 49, 56
Gulf Stream, Franklin's experiments
   on, 46

Hamilton, Alexander, 26–27,
   120–22

indigenous knowledge, 27–29
industrial espionage, 26–27
industrialization, 125–26
industrial research, 111, 124–25
information technology, 14, 15, 29
innovation, 4, 36
intellectual property rights, 1, 2, 7,
   9, 37, 43; commercialization of,
   6, 11, 33, 110–11; constitutional
   basis for, 79–82; in developing
   countries, 24–27, 112–15;
   economic value of, 11, 12, 32, 33;
   effects on democracy of, 137;
   impact on prosperity of, 3, 11; as
   incentives for creativity, 11; as
   intangible assets, 10; knowledge
   and, 4; management of, 2, 6, 7,
   9, 10, 11, 31, 32; as policy tools,
   136–38; political impact of, 3, 51;
   promoting access to, 5, 6, 10–12,
   30, 37, 81; public benefit of, 4,
   33, 51

international technology transfer,
   24–27
Internet, 13–14, 16, 29, 31, 41
interoperability, 77
inventions: collaborative
   development of, 132–33;
   commercialization of, 6, 23–24,
   74–76; economic development
   from, 24; economic incentives for,
   6, 23–24; impact on social order
   of, 66; improvements in, 66,
   68–69, 76, 87–88
inventors, 53, 65–78, 74–76, 80
iron bridge technology, 57–58
Isaacks, Jacob, 72–77, 108–9

knowledge: applied, 1, 4,
   49–52, 71–72; as basis for
   self-sufficiency and democracy,
   3, 5; dissemination of, 4, 6, 10,
   11, 22, 50–51; improving human
   condition through, 3, 4, 38,
   49–52; networks of, 5, 39–40,
   42–43; pooling, 39–40, 50–51;
   proprietary rights of, 10, 29–32,
   39, 41–42; as a public asset, 51;
   sharing, 22, 27–29, 31, 35, 37–43,
   50–51, 52 53, 71, 114–15
Knox, Henry, 82

land measurement system, 120
Lewis and Clark expedition, 47–49
licenses, 14, 103, 106, 107
lightning rod, 81
Locke, John, 62
Lunar Society of Birmingham, 64

Madison, James, 57, 80, 85, 97
Martin, Thomas, 68
mathematics, 68, 123
McPherson, Isaac, 39, 104

scientific (*continued*)
   inquiry, 12, 43, 48, 56–57; scout, 26; synthesizer, 60–61
Shapley, Harlow, 61
smallpox, 61
Small, William, 63
soil, observations of recorded, 48
Statute of Anne (1709), 35
Statute of Monopolies (1624), 83–84
steam engine technology, 102
submarines, 69

Taylor, John, 68
technical standards, 115–24
technology commercialization, 6–7, 101–2, 106–7, 109–11, 132–33
Thailand, 26
threshing machine, 68
torpedoes, 69
trademarks, 1, 9, 10, 32; abandonment of, 34; generic, 34
trade secrets, 1, 9, 30, 32
transits of Venus, measurement of, 58
Trumbull, John, 62

U.S. Congress, 72, 73, 103, 119, 120, 122
U.S. Constitution, 79, 85, 88, 120

U.S. Library of Congress, 13
U.S. Military Academy at West Point, 45–46
U.S. Navy, 72
University of Virginia, 44–45, 51, 68
utility, requirement of, 30, 86

vaccinations, 61
Vaughan, Benjamin, 97
Virginia General Assembly, 37
Von Humboldt, Alexander, 60

Waterhouse, Benjamin, 61
waterproof material, 65–66
Watt, James, 6, 31, 97, 110, 124–25
weights and measures, 116–19
wheel cipher, 70
Whitney, Eli, 6, 110
Willard, Joseph, 64
Williams, Jonathan, 46
Williamson, Hugh, 91
Wistar, Caspar, 48, 72, 74, 113
wood-burning distillation, 72–77
Wright, Orville and Wilbur, 124, 128
Wythe, George, 38, 63

Young, Thomas, 60–61
YouTube, 12